Tactics of Hope

Tactics of Hope

The Public Turn in English Composition

Paula Mathieu

Boynton/Cook Publishers, Inc.
HEINEMANN
Portsmouth, NH

Boynton/Cook Publishers, Inc.
A subsidiary of Reed Elsevier Inc.
361 Hanover Street
Portsmouth, NH 03801–3912
www.boyntoncook.com

Offices and agents throughout the world

The author and publisher wish to thank those who have generously given permission to reprint borrowed material:

Excerpt from *City Comp: Identities, Spaces, Practices*, edited by Bruce McComisky and Cynthia Ryan, the State University of New York Press. Copyright © 2003 by the State University of New York. All rights reserved.

"Questions of Time: Publishing and Group Identity in the *StreetWise* Writers Group" by Paula Mathieu, Karen Westmoreland, Michael Ibrahem, and Curly Cohen from *Writing Groups Inside and Outside the Classroom*, edited by Beverly J. Moss, Nels P. Highberg, and Melissa Nicolas. Copyright © 2004 by Lawrence Erlbaum Associates, Inc.

Library of Congress Cataloging-in-Publication Data
Mathieu, Paula.
    Tactics of hope : street life and the public turn in English composition / Paula Mathieu.
        p. cm.
    Includes bibliographical references and index.
    ISBN 0-86709-578-4 (alk. paper)
    1. English language—Composition and exercises—Study and teaching—Social aspects. 2. English language—Rhetoric—Study and teaching—Social aspects. 3. Written communication—Study and teaching—Social aspects. 4. Report writing—Study and teaching—Social aspects. 5. Popular culture. 6. Community life. 7. Street life.   I. Title.

PE1404.M37 2005
808'.042'071—dc22   2004030672

Editor: James Strickland
Production service: Argosy
Production coordination: Vicki Kasabian
Cover design: Joni Doherty
Typesetter: Argosy
Manufacturing: Steve Bernier

Printed in the United States of America on acid-free paper
09 08 07 06 05 DA 1 2 3 4 5

Contents

Acknowledgments

If any part of me didn't fully know beforehand, this project has taught me once and for all that all writing is collaborative. For this project, the advice, counseling, and prodding of many friends was essential; and I owe them all my deep gratitude.

This book would not be possible without the ideas, feedback, and support of the amazing people whom I am fortunate to know and have worked with at street papers around the world, especially Tim Harris, Curly Cohen, Marc Goldfinger, Tom Boland, Fran Czajkowski, Megan Mahoney, Lisa Maclean, Mel Young, Anitra Freeman, Charles Ferguson, Cindy Carlson, Layla Mewburn, and particularly Alex Tsouvalas.

I have deep appreciation and esteem for Diana George, Howard Zinn, and Sandra Andrews, who generously agreed to share their time and wisdom with me.

Many friends and colleagues helped me complete this work by listening, reading, and offering feedback. My deepest thanks are owed to Frank Farmer, David Stacey, and Tobi Jacobi whose feedback and support were essential at key moments of my writing. Many other colleagues are owed a debt of gratitude, including Annie Knepler, James Sosnoski, Tim Lindgren, Staci Shultz, Robert Stanton, Derek Owens, Hill Taylor, Dan Collins, Stuart Brown, Martha Hincks, Robin Lydenberg, Ti Bodenheimer, Lad Tobin, and Rhonda Frederick. Thanks to Elizabeth Bernardi for editorial help, and to Amy Warfield for rescuing the scan of my photo image. Thanks to the entire production staff at Heinemann and Argosy Publishing. A special thanks to Jim Strickland, for being a supportive editor and a living example of hope. Finally, I owe my love and deepest gratitude to my family and friends, who keep me sane and know not to take me too seriously.

Introduction

"We're Not Cops, We're from the University"

In the 1992 horror film *Candyman*, two aspiring academics, Helen Lyle (Virginia Madsen) and Bernadette Walsh (Kasi Lemmons), land on a thesis topic that leads them to Chicago's Cabrini Green public housing project in search of data about a local urban legend. As only Hollywood can, this film depicts doctoral research in what appears to be an Urban Legends Department, filled with faculty lecturing to packed classes. Receiving a tip from a black cleaning woman on campus, the two graduate students rush to Cabrini Green in hopes of debunking the legend of the Candyman,[1] which the project residents purportedly believe. Without invitation or permission, the two enter one of the high-rise buildings and climb several flights of the stairs (the elevator is of course not working), walking past graffitied walls and many African American residents. Lyle, who is white, and Walsh, who is black, are both dressed smartly in long coats, slacks, and heels; they express relief when the building's residents mistake them for the "5-0" (police).

Once upstairs, they enter an abandoned apartment, the scene of an alleged Candyman attack, search it, and take photographs as data for their research. A next-door neighbor, Ann-Marie McCoy (Vanessa Williams), a young African American woman dressed for work as a hospital orderly and carrying an infant, stands in the doorway and confronts them. "What you all doing in there?" she asks.

Although happy to be mistaken for the police a moment earlier, Lyle now seeks to assure McCoy of the opposite, saying, "We're not cops; we're from the university."

McCoy seems annoyed and says so: "Well, you don't belong here, lady. You don't belong going through people's apartments and things."

Lyle then walks toward her, speaking deliberately: "My name is Helen Lyle and this is Bernadette Walsh. We're doing a thesis." She says the word "thesis" slowly to draw out the syllables, underscoring its foreignness in the dingy, abandoned apartment where they stand. "And we were wondering if we could just talk to you for a few minutes. Here, this is my card." Not unlike a cop flashing her badge, Lyle presents a business card that confirms her affiliation with a different state apparatus, the local university. Lyle's calm confidence is offset by the uncomfortable demeanor of Walsh, her African American research partner, who quietly apologizes to McCoy and unconvincingly urges Lyle to the door.

McCoy remains suspicious and critical: "So you say you're doing a study. What you gonna study? That we're all bad? That we steal? We gang bang? We're all on drugs, right?" And when she begrudgingly agrees to talk to the researchers, she adds, "You know, whites don't never come here except to cause us a problem."

Lyle confidently replies, "Believe me; that's not what we want to do." As any horror fan knows, her assured tone, which is not unfamiliar to university faculty, inevitably foreshadows death and disaster. And in the ensuing scenes of *Candyman*, horrible things do happen, especially to Lyle and Walsh.

Despite its sometimes cartoonish and often very grim horror, *Candyman* offers a useful scene for excavating the tacit assumptions underlying much university work in the streets outside of campus. Lyle caricatures an academic entitled by race and cultural capital who launches thoughtlessly into unfamiliar streets and buildings, focused solely on *her* work, damn the consequences for others or even herself. Without any relationship or even permission, she embarks on her project and expects others outside of campus to help. She has no understanding of McCoy's mistrust and apprehension or a sense of why people might be suspicious of working with universities.

The film resonates with me personally because it was filmed in Chicago (where I grew up) on the very campus where I did my graduate work. It was released the year I began getting involved in local writing projects outside of campus. And like the thesis of the fictional researchers, my work on occasion brought me to Cabrini Green. So, for me, this unattractive Hollywood portrayal of a graduate student in the street landed *literally* a little too close to home.

I wanted to dismiss Helen Lyle as a Hollywood distortion. Clearly "we"—real-life teachers, writers, and scholars who connect academic teaching and research with local communities—know better. Or is it too easy to feel superior to the fictional researchers? Perhaps these Hollywood doppelgangers resemble real academics and students more than we want to admit.

While obviously exaggerated, this scene in *Candyman* highlights several problems that can arise when even well-intentioned academics or students hit the streets. Lyle and Walsh meant no harm. They had a research plan (at least the Hollywood version of a research plan—they talked with faculty and went to the library, once). Their interest in the urban legends circulated by residents of Cabrini Green would have added to a scholarly body of work. Unfortunately, their plan and actions assumed and relied upon cooperation of Cabrini residents, who had no voice in the planning or decision to go ahead with this project. Absent an ongoing relationship and a shared vision of work with those in the streets, academics and students can too easily create horror stories of our own, filled with misunderstandings, missed opportunities, and bitterness.

Universities in the Streets

Many disciplines within the university, especially English composition, now foster initiatives that send students, teachers, and researchers out of the classroom and into "the streets."[2] Too often, teachers send students where they themselves seldom go. Or they might plan their research and teaching agendas first and then seek out suitable "sites" in the street to do that work. At best, academics ask local agencies how they or their students can help meet agency needs. But how often is our asking much better than that of the researchers in *Candyman*?

When students and teachers move from the classroom to the streets, many questions arise or should arise: How well do we know our local communities and how well known are we in them? Are those outside the university eager or reluctant to work with us? How prepared are we to go through the process of learning how to understand and respond to local needs? Do we know how to frame questions in useful ways and listen for answers, even ones we might not like? How well do we understand how public discourse operates in our communities? How well can we present or represent local issues in our classrooms? In short, how well can academics see beyond our own good intentions to assess how our work resonates with those in the streets? As the field of composition turns its attention more and more to local street life, teachers and scholars will need to examine more questions like these in order to evaluate how our missions, projects, research, writing, and teaching play to those in the streets whom we purport to serve.

What the ill-fated academics in *Candyman* failed to recognize is that place matters, as does time. Moving from the university to the streets means that the rules that prevail in the classroom or the dean's office no longer apply. As academics increasingly seek "placements" in the community for their students or for their own research, a need to understand the politics and dynamics of place—as well as time—are paramount.

Composition as a field has begun taking serious account of the spaces and spatial politics involved in the research and pedagogy of teaching writing.[3] While important theoretical research seeks to understand street locations as unique entities, more work is necessary to appreciate how the streets differ from institutional spaces like universities and schools. Rather than relying on the strategies that usually work in classrooms and on campuses, academics in the streets need to understand the spatial politics around them and call on the tactics available in a given time and place.[4]

A Word on the Word *Street*

As I discuss in Chapter 1, a wide range of teaching practices and campus initiatives bring the work of college students and faculty beyond the boundaries of classroom and campus walls. But what can we call that beyond space? Describing or naming "out there" has proven difficult and theoretically unsatisfactory for many writers and scholars. I have chosen *street* as the metonymic reference point for those places outside of universities and schools that have become sites of research, outreach, service, or local learning. *Street* may refer to a specific neighborhood, community center, school, or local nonprofit organization. Like all the other possible terms (such as *community*, *sites of service*, *contact zones*, *outreach site*, etc.), *street* is a problematic term, but it is one whose problems, I hope, help illuminate the difficulties associated with academic outreach. Before discussing *street*, I will briefly mention why the other terms seem more problematic.

Joseph Harris chose *community* as one of the key terms reflective of dominant pedagogical approaches to composition since the mid-1960s. But as Harris points out, *community* connotes a misleading sense of unity. In *Keywords*, Raymond Williams describes *community* as the "warmly persuasive" term that "unlike all other terms of social organization (*state, nation, society*) . . . never [seems] to be used unfavourably" (76). Because of the persuasive warmth of *community*, it is difficult to see such a site as uncommunal, complex, or conflictual. In addition, as Harris shows, *community* can mean any group, inside or outside the academy, thus making terms like *community literacy* or *community-based writing* ambiguous or possibly euphemistic.

Mary Louise Pratt's nuanced configuration, *contact zone*, offers a theoretically rich term, which is useful in explicating the dynamics of a place.[5] However, *contact zone*, like *community*, is a broad term that lacks a specific geographic referent, in that contact zones can exist in classrooms as well as in streets, historical periods, etc. Plus, *contact zone* carries a whiff of academic jargon that makes its practical usefulness questionable. For example, "I'm doing research in my local contact zone" is a sentence determined not to roll off the tongue comfortably. Nor is it likely that most people would appreciate having their local neighborhood referred to as a *contact zone,* which sounds similar to *combat zone,* especially to residents in the Boston area, where I now work.[6] Alternative terms such as *non-academic, outreach,* and *extracurricular* describe "the out-there places" in relation to what they are not—the university—which invokes the binary *town-gown,* assigning the university as the normal term of comparison and relegating the town to relational status.

Likewise, describing a location as a *site of service* reverberates in a range of troubling ways. Service implies "good works," and often calls up visions of unequal power, with an individual in a superior position of strength helping another who is presumed weaker *or* deficient. In a different way, some worry that for young people the term *service* now often names mandatory "volunteer" work they must do in schools or calls up images of the "court-ordered community service" that movie and rock stars must carry out, mostly for drug crimes.[7] The concept "service," like that of excellence,[8] is an empty signifier, one which posits the existence of a generic category of something positive and useful—which would require a neutral and uninterested political point from which to judge.

I somewhat reluctantly adopt *street* as the spatial metaphor for the destination of academic outreach and service learning, because although it is also problematic, its problems seem generative. *Street* implies *urban,* which itself has been considered a racist euphemism for *black.* "Urban music," for example, is marketing code for "black music."[9] "Urban renewal," studies show, has been used euphemistically to signify removal of black residents from neighborhoods to pave the way for gentrification (e.g., Shareef 2001). *Street* carries connotations of homelessness, gangs, and poverty. Wealthy people tend not to spend much time in the streets, and when they do it's often within regulated and semiprivatized spaces, such as gated communities or sidewalks in gentrified neighborhoods.

As universities create local and public initiatives, aren't the *streets* largely where we and our students are heading to read, to write, and to serve? Prisons, homeless shelters, learning centers in poor neighborhoods, community newspapers, and small nonprofits tend to be where students work in service-learning projects. When teachers bring "local life" into the classroom, it is more often ethnic literature, ethnographies of people living in marginalized situations, and theories of subordinated groups than critical studies of powerful groups like CEOs, country clubs, or slumlords. The lives of lower-income people tend to be more public or accessible to academics than the lives of the wealthy. In other words, it is much easier to gain street access than boardroom access. At the same time, however, use of the word *street* is tricky, especially from the computer of an academic; it risks replicating the racist rhetoric of urban renewal that it seeks to critique by viewing the streets as a monolithic entity. Many locations in neighborhoods are defined explicitly as sites that are *not* part of the streets, like centers that offer positive alternatives for youth.

With increasing interest in public initiatives, writing instruction today is deeply implicated in complications of race and class and institutional power, and the ethical problems are complex. In choosing the term *street*, I certainly do not solve these problems but rather seek to continually remind myself and others that taking our teaching and learning to the streets has serious implications.

Goals of This Book

The central argument of *Tactics of Hope* is that the field of English composition has taken a turn to the streets, which has broad implications for the organization and assessment of writing, teaching, and research. I argue that thus far composition's public initiatives have relied primarily on *strategic logics*—proceeding as if the university were the controlling institution determining movements and interactions. A strategic orientation seeks to control spaces and create institutional relationships with an "other" in the community. Strategic development of initiatives, like service learning, seek objective calculations of success and thus rely on spatial markers like sustainability and measurable student outcomes as guidelines of success.

The problem lies in the fact that universities or other educational institutions do not have strategic control over the streets. Try as one might to create "clients" or "partners" in the name of institutional partnerships, the everyday workings of street life are more complex, with multiple sources of power (Harper et al. 2003). The institutional reach of universities cannot contain street life within a strategic orientation. The more we try to institutionalize the relationships between universities and neighboring streets and communities, the farther we stray from a rhetorically responsive engagement that seeks timely partnerships, which acknowledge the ever-changing spatial terrain, temporal opportunities, and voices of individuals. The more we rely on strategic models, which seek stability instead of specificity, the more marginalized and disregarded will be the everyday voices and opinions of those in the streets and neighborhoods we seek to serve. The following chapters recount several horror stories—not from film but real life—that illustrate the gaps that can occur between a university's understanding of its own work and its reception in the streets outside of campus.

In opposition to a strategic orientation, I argue on behalf of a *tactical orientation*, which understands both temporal and spatial politics.

University-community partnerships, in a tactical orientation, would necessarily be rhetorical and changing. Rather than scientific measures of success, street initiatives would operate situationally, grounded in both time and place.

Adopting a tactical orientation in a university setting means letting go of comfortable claims of certainty and accepting the contingent and vexed nature of our actions. A tactical orientation needs to be grounded in hope, not cast in naïve or passive terms, but hope as a critical, active, dialectical engagement between the insufficient present and possible, alternative futures—a dialogue composed of many voices.

This book examines a trend within higher education to connect with local communities, and in doing so, seeks to amplify the voices of those who have worked with university courses but are not of or in the university: people in local neighborhoods, communities, and streets who accommodate, become involved with, and with any luck, benefit from university outreach and publicly oriented courses. I do not claim that the information I present here is either exhaustive or necessarily generalizable; rather, I have compiled a collection of memories, interviews, and personal reflections of various nonprofit workers and activists (including myself). This book acts as a metonymic gesture to stand in for the many, many voices teachers and scholars need to be hearing and learning from if we decide to venture into the streets.

In Chapter 1, "Composition in the Streets," I catalogue the various initiatives through which writing instructors, students, and researchers have connected with the streets outside of campus, which together constitutes what I call a *public turn* for composition studies. I outline various initiatives that seem to me part of this public turn, including bringing classroom writing to the streets via public writing, bringing street life into the classroom through course content, sending students into the streets through service learning, and encouraging teachers/writers/scholars to connect their work to the streets. I explore the history and motivations of this public turn in composition and argue that despite this radical changing of places, we continue to rely on strategic rather than tactical guidelines for organizing and assessing our work. Beyond critiquing this approach, I offer an alternative configuration for examining and understanding street initiatives as *tactics of hope*, by relying on theories of tactics by Michel de Certeau and writings on hope by several theorists, including Ernst Bloch.

Chapter 2, "Writing in the Streets," explores public writing in classrooms and argues that our teaching can be informed and enriched by public writing already occurring in the streets. Through the examples of writers at community newspapers and activist organizations, I outline public writing as tactical and seek ways to connect lessons of tactical writing to classroom projects.

Chapter 3, "Street Life in the Classroom," examines university classes that include local issues and literature as course content. As a case study for this chapter, I discuss a course I have taught, Literatures of Homelessness, in which I have relied on the help and advice of local community activists.

Chapter 4, "Students in the Streets," reports some of the apprehension and dissatisfaction many community members feel toward university-initiated service learning projects. I argue that the push to institutionalize service learning, which dominates the current literature, risks further alienating community members by relying on strategic rather than tactical measures for design and assessment. I offer examples of tactical service projects that may not be as large or sustainable as strategic programs but may be more accountable.

The book concludes with "Teachers/Writers/Scholars in the Streets," which examines recent calls to expand the public role of English language and literature scholars and argues that, despite this interest, academic scholarship is largely evaluated by strategic, disciplinary measures. I share the story of a community group embittered by a partnership that gave them nothing but helped an academic improve his publishing profile. To counter this horror story, I share examples of three personal academic heroes who, to me, embody tactical views of working and rely on hope to continue each day. I conclude the book with a meditation on hope and how it can inform our work in the streets.

The Streets Where I Live

Before moving to Chapter 1, I want to share something about the streets where I live and work. For the past seven years I have worked with one foot in the university, as a graduate student and now assistant professor, and the other in the nonprofit sector, as a teacher, writer, editor, and administrator at two street newspapers, which are organizations that provide income and a public voice to people who are homeless or living in poverty. As a graduate student, I studied composition theory at the same time I was teaching writing to homeless men and women and receiving offers from local universities to create service-learning partnerships. As an assistant professor, I left my hometown and relocated to a new city and tried to initiate work at a different street paper, defining new roles and projects based on local needs and cultures. During these years, I have designed and taught university-writing courses at two very different institutions (an urban state university and an affluent Jesuit university) that engage social issues both in the classroom and in the streets.

Working both for small nonprofits and universities, I have been able to see the public gestures of writing faculty and students from two angles simultaneously. This double perspective has allowed me to see the limitations and promise of writing and service goals as articulated by the university. I have also seen how local realities often require that ideas about writing, pedagogy, and service be defined differently than in universities.

On Street Papers, Gingerbread Men, and Hope

The most important lessons about writing I have learned come from working with writers who are or have been homeless. Everything I have know about teaching writing and community partnerships has been filtered through, informed, challenged, and extended by my seven-years' work with the international grassroots movement of street newspapers. More than 100 street papers operate as independent media organizations in 27 countries on six continents. Built on the principle of self-help, street papers give people living in poverty the chance to earn an income by selling high-quality, alternative magazines and newspapers to the reading public. Many street papers also provide an outlet for socially excluded people to articulate their views of the world and to claim a voice in the public media.

While acting independently, most of the world's street papers belong to a common network, the International Network of Street Papers (INSP).[10] The INSP supports its member papers as they create social businesses that aim "to alleviate poverty and build a just, civil society in the world." INSP articulates its vision as both local and global, by "changing the world one street paper at a time."

A typical street paper operates this way: A person who is living in poverty or needing work can come to a street-paper office, attend an orientation session, and receive a badge[11] and a number of free papers to sell. Subsequently, vendors purchase copies of the paper at a reduced price (usually a quarter to half of the cover price) and sell them to the public at the cover price—usually a dollar or two—keeping the proceeds. Street papers provide a modest job to anyone wanting to work, and also work for longer-term systemic change through international lobbying efforts and the pages of their newspapers and magazines. INSP has recently gained consultative status with the United Nations, is creating an international news service, and takes part in international summits like the World Social Forum and World Economic Forum.

I would like to pass along a story to you, a story told to me by Layla Mewburn from *Big Issue Scotland*, who heard it from Robert Sztarovics from *Novy Prostor* in Prague, which as he tells it, is based on a lesson he learned from his mother. It's a story that figured centrally in the planning of the 2003 INSP conference in Prague, where I retold the story to a plenary session of roughly 70 delegates from street papers in 27 countries. Perhaps the story has been repeated since then. It describes the spirit of the street-paper movement, which is not based on charity but on tactical projects that create social opportunities. This story—and all my experiences with street papers—has helped clarify my understanding of creating university partnerships that I call *tactical projects;* it has also taught me a great deal about hope.

The teller of the story—Robert, Layla, me, or you—begins by drawing the figure of a body. It looks a bit like a gingerbread man:

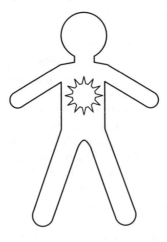

This is a body. It can be the body of an individual—a student, a homeless person, a university president—or it can represent a collective body, such as a class, a group of homeless writers, a local community group, or the street-paper movement. The sun in the middle represents the body's essence, or soul. The larger part of the body, outside the sun, represents incompleteness, problems, challenges, difficulties, failings—all that is wrong with the homeless person or student or local community. The sun (no matter how big or small) represents all that is perfect, funny, creative, accomplished, skillful—everything that is working in that person or community or organization. No matter how difficult one's life, no matter how many problems a community has encountered, there remains a vibrant section of creative and positive energy. Someone who is addicted to heroin, who is homeless, who may even steal to get drugs, can be a gifted poet and storyteller. A homeless street-paper vendor may struggle with reading or emotional problems but can play soccer, grow to become part of a team, and travel around the world to play in the Homeless World Cup Tournament.[12]

Charity—or what I later describe as a *problem orientation*—focuses on the areas of a body that need fixing or ameliorating, whether it's alcoholism or misplaced modifiers, lack of job skills or an inability to create acceptable academic discourse. The goal of charity or a problem orientation is to decrease the prevalence of a given problem. It often involves strategic initiatives and long-term plans.

Alternately, street papers—and many other community groups and teachers—employ what I could call a *tactical orientation*: They focus on creating projects that emphasize the part of the soul that is creative, competent, vibrant. Rather than making long-term efforts to fix problems, this approach seeks *tactical* uses of time and resources to celebrate, encourage, or develop those aspects of a body that are already working. This approach often takes the form not of long-term problem amelioration but limited-term projects. Vendors sell street papers at will, beginning and leaving as they choose. The stories covered in newspapers last a week, two weeks, a month. One project is incomplete in itself and must build on another. All of the projects at street papers are rooted in bettering the lives of those living in poverty. Some are silly or strange, such as the Homeless World Cup or Not Your Mama's Bus Tour,[13] and others are serious and practical, like a toner recycling business to employ street-paper vendors in Uruguay or the creation of a Global Street News Service. Projects are locally defined and action oriented. They arise from a familiarity with a situation and a desire for a creative response.

These projects provide limited direct benefits: usually informing readers or giving an individual a small income or an interesting experience. But tactical projects also operate in the realm of the indirect and the possible. Many things *may* happen in the course of doing projects. Someone may decide to kick heroin. A reader may change how he or she feels about the homeless man asleep on the corner. Someone may finally learn word processing or improve academic literacy skills. Certain problems may disappear or decrease, through the act of doing something else. But then again, they might not.

Projects by their *tactical* orientation are limited, and as a result the claims for them must be limited as well. When completed, projects accomplish only themselves—the printing and selling of a newspaper or magazine, the completion of a specific campaign, the publishing of a collection of writing, the staging of a soccer match. In the face of mounting global poverty and increasing gaps between rich and poor, such projects are rather insufficient. They immediately demand more projects, new ideas, continued innovations, and sustained campaigns. I find this tactical orientation both exciting and deeply humbling, one that is grounded in *hope* but in a critical manifestation of hope, one that is based in action and proceeds with eyes open.

As scholarship about the teaching of writing increasingly concerns itself with the streets and communities outside our classrooms and campuses, most of this writing continues to work from the inside out, describing what research, theory, and pedagogy from the university can tell us about working in the streets. In this book, I try to reverse the tide and describe some of the theory, teaching, and writing projects that have been working in the streets where I have lived and to connect that knowledge with the questions our field has been asking about its public commitments. Street papers are just one kind of organization that can provide valuable lessons to us if we reverse our camera lens; instead of looking, studying, and examining outside our schools and universities, we can let those with whom we work outside of campus reflect and speak to us.

Like most teachers I know, I contend regularly with questions of the ethics and efficacy of my work as a teacher and scholar. I have written this book not because I am an expert in community partnerships, but because I have realized that, with each year's experience, new questions and complications arise when assessing the value of the work I do. By seeing my teaching and research as *tactics of hope*, I am able to seek new insights by reminding myself to acknowledge limitations while working to find more productive and innovative projects— primarily by asking and listening to those in the streets and in my classroom. By presenting my views and the insights of a range of community members with whom I have worked, I do not offer any final words; rather, I offer a range of ethical and practical questions to consider regarding the public turn in composition.

Notes

1. For those interested in the details of the urban legend, the Internet Movie Database summarizes it this way: ". . . the Candyman (Tony Todd) was once an ex-slave-turned-artist name Daniel Robitaille, who had an affair with his client's daughter. Robitaille's right hand was sawn off, he was covered in honey, and stung to death by bees. If anyone says the word 'Candyman' five times in a mirror, he'll appear behind that person, a bloody hook as a replacement for his hand, and kill him. A series of unsolved murders is happening in the Cabrini Green projects and Helen is using this to help with her paper" (http://imdb.com/title/tt0103919/plotsummary).

2. See the next section for more on this term.

3. E.g., Reynolds; Porter et al.; McComiskey and Ryan; and Di Leo, Jacobs, and Lee. See also Chapter 1.

4. See Chapter 1 for an overview of strategies and tactics.

5. See Cushman and Emmons for outreach work focused on contact zones.

6. An area in Boston near Chinatown was formerly known as the "Combat Zone." Decried by city officials for its "adult entertainment" and "illicit activities," the neighborhood was eventually rezoned and gentrified. See http://www.ci.boston.ma.us/boston400/main.asp?ID=435.

7. For a discussion of this issue, see the Working Group on National and Community Service at http://www.ysa.org/wp/wp1202/wp121702a.html.

8. Harkin, in (2002) has spoken about "excellence" as an empty signifier that dictates the game of higher education. Also see Readings; Aronowitz; Downing, Hurlbert, and Mathieu.

9. See, for example, commentary in Guardian's music news at http://www.guardian.co.uk/arts/news/story/0,11711,840380,00.html.

10. For more information on street papers, see http://www.street-papers.com and http://www.nasna.org. From 2003 to 2005, I have served as the sole North American member of the INSP Executive Committee, a body elected by the delegates at annual conventions.

11. In many cities, street papers have faced legal battles to allow vendors to sell their papers on the streets. Issuing an official badge has become a necessity in many cities to make newspaper vending legal. Many vendors worldwide, however, continue to contend with police harassment.

12. The Homeless World Cup is a street-soccer tournament that began as a joking idea between two delegates at an INSP conference, debating whose paper's vendors would win in a soccer tournament. Created by the International Network of Street Papers, this small idea has grown into a major annual event that was held for the first time in Graz, Austria, in the summer of 2003. Homeless men and women, many of whom have never played soccer or traveled internationally, represent their country in a tournament of 18 countries. Thus far, this strange little idea has brought many secondary benefits to the men and women who have participated. For more information, see http://www.streetsoccer.org.

13. See Chapter 2.

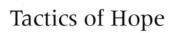

Tactics of Hope

One

Composition in the Streets

The "Public Turn" in Composition Studies

Composition is hitting the streets, and has been for some time now. University writing specialists are working outside the walls of universities at increasing rates, in part because of political or pedagogical aims, and in part because of shifting university mandates. Service learning, community literacy, and public writing are just some of the names given to a broadening array of outreach initiatives that find writing teachers or their students working and writing in neighborhood centers in addition to university classrooms. In addition to this move outward, many composition teachers bring issues from the streets into the classroom. An example that illustrates both aspects of this trend is the 2002 Conference on College and Composition and Communication, with its theme "Connecting the Text and the Street":

> We must teach [students] to use the texts they already own and to compose new texts in ways that affect the quality of lives in the "street," in all those sites beyond the classroom—offices, hospitals, daycare centers, workplaces, prisons, homes, and homeless shelters. Our writing classes, not constrained by the need to cover a specific subject matter, remain ideal sites in which to develop such literacies.

Writing instruction conceived this way goes beyond notions of academic competence to encompass discursive projects in many areas of community life. This *public turn* in composition studies more generally asks teachers to connect the writing that students and they themselves do with "real world" texts, events, or exigencies.[1] At the heart of this call to the streets is a desire for writing to enter civic debates;[2] for street life to enter classrooms through a focus on local, social issues;[3] for

1

students to hit the streets by performing service,[4] and for teachers and scholars to conduct activist or community-grounded research.[5]

While much has been written individually about these initiatives—writing in the streets (or public writing), street life in the classroom, students in the streets, and teachers/writers/scholars in the streets—when taken together, they could be considered a significant turn in composition studies toward the public and the streets. Many composition initiatives today could be relevantly discussed under more than one of these categories, while other current work in composition lies altogether outside this interest in the public realm. While imperfect and incomplete, this sketch provides an overview of the range of relationships now existing between university writing classes and the streets around them.

Writing in the Streets

Public Writing in Classrooms

Christian Weisser connects the history of composition studies to an interest in public writing in *Moving Beyond Academic Discourse*. He overviews the work of several composition scholars who research public writing, including Susan Wells, John Trimbur, and Evelyn Ashton Jones. Like Wells, Weisser grounds theoretical interest in public-sphere debates in theories like those of Jurgen Habermas and his critics, including Richard Sennett, Nancy Fraser, and Oskar Negt and Alexander Kluge. Weisser argues that those interested in teaching public writing would benefit from a theoretical understanding of Habermas' optimistic construct of the public sphere and important criticisms of his work, which in different ways call for greater attention to the attenuated spaces where people appeal to and create alternative publics. Weisser asserts that debates about how notions of public-sphere participation is formed, critiqued, and contested should be central to notions of teaching composition.

Weisser notes that when many teachers think of public writing assignments, they imagine a letter to the editor. Such one-off assignments unrelated to a specific inquiry or ongoing debate can be less than satisfactory, as Diana George explains: "When I first started teaching writing, the idea of public discourse we had in our mind was to write a letter to the editor. But you'd really get discouraged if sending letters was your only aim. Letters are either not published, cut, or sandwiched between two other letters that seem crazed" (2004). Theorists like George, Wells, and Rosa Eberly have added theoretical depth to discussions of public writing by acknowledging the complex and conflicted terrain for which students must write, while making calls for the field to investigate writing, as it takes place, in local public venues.[6]

Web-Based Publishing

The expansiveness of the World Wide Web allows for a relatively quick and inexpensive global readership for student writing. A third of the essays in *Public Works,* edited by Emily Isaacs and Phoebe Jackson, focuses on virtual publics and raises questions about the ethics of Web-based publishing. Charles Moran, for example, argues that the Web increases the ethical and practical complexities of writing with a public focus. Gian Pagnucci and Nick Mauriello demonstrate some of these ethical dilemmas, discussing students who fear that their Web-based writing will be stolen, misunderstood, or may expose them in painful or even dangerous ways. Despite these concerns, many teachers rely on Web-based technologies to create virtual spaces of local community or make connections with nonvirtual local neighborhoods.[7]

Street Life in the Writing Classroom

Social and Cultural Issues in the Classroom

Robert Yagelski and Scott Leonard's collection *The Relevance of English: Teaching That Matters in Students' Lives* is a recent entry in the ongoing conversation about the ways in which English studies can be "relevant (or irrelevant) to students in an increasingly complex and interconnected world" (324). Contributors to that volume offer a range of answers to questions of relevance, some which include forays into public discussions on campus, online, and in towns. Contributors to *Beyond English Inc.,* such as James Zebroski and Daniel Collins, explore how economic demands shape possibilities for meaningful course offerings in writing in, respectively, a graduate program in rhetoric and a community college focused on vocational education (Downing et al. 2002).

Many teachers answer the question of relevance by bringing into the classroom issues of local importance or political polarity. Cultural studies have ushered in an interest in popular culture, asking students to write about relevant texts and artifacts from their local subcultures, like musical lyrics, codes of conduct at the local dojo, or advertising in a magazine. Many composition teachers today encourage students' civic participation and local engagement with issues such as American identity, race, gender, political discourse, or local legal cases and debates.[8] In such classes, issues of power and rhetoric arise: competing ideologies, clarifying the political role of the teacher, and seeking a rhetoric that does not alienate nor efface the political views of students and staff.[9]

Sustainability and Places of Writing

Street life is finding its way into writing classrooms as students bring it in themselves, from hometowns and local sources. Growing out of text-based cultural studies and ethnographic research practices, some composition classrooms take on issues of public concern by asking students to write about and understand places where they live. A rise in interest in "place-based" writing is occurring, with more work being published in ecocomposition and sustainability.[10] Through an interest in sustainability as a framing justification for a writing course, Derek Owens (2001) constructs writing pedagogies that send students out into their neighborhoods to record stories about local places and people by drawing on techniques of narrative, cultural studies analysis, historical research, and oral history. Nancy Mack (2002) encourages students to build multigenre, multimedia research projects that draw on their families and histories. In *Letters for the Living*, Michael Blitz and Claude Mark Hurlbert describe the writing projects of their students (from New York City and rural Pennsylvania, respectively), who swap neighborhood stories and writing, and produce books about local experiences. In many universities, place-based courses have become central to the first-year writing program; websites publicly catalogue the place-oriented writings of local students.[11] Place-based writing courses that focus on neighborhood spaces ask students to create meaningful and often lasting documents of those spaces and blur the lines between classrooms and the streets. Increasing amounts of scholarship link questions of pedagogy to specificities of place.[12]

Students in the Streets

Service Learning

Service learning in composition combines a writing class with work at a community site. Advocates of service learning praise it for motivating students, reinvigorating composition curricula, and "rearticulat[ing] the university as part of, not opposed to, local communities" (Adler-Kassner et al. 1997, 4). Service learning has gained greater institutional acceptance over the years through scholarship that has touted its success. It has been shown to offer active ways for students to participate in their communities and solve classroom dilemmas, such as "empty assignment syndrome" (Brack and Hall 1997, 143) and "unreal rhetorical situations" (Heilker 1997, 71). An increasing amount of scholarship critiquing and theorizing service learning is being circulated in the standard professional journals and in new venues, such as the service-learning journal *Reflections.*

Community-Based Literacy

Related to but distinct from service learning are initiatives described as community literacy.[13] Community literacy, as defined by Peck et al., is "a search for an alternative discourse," with an aim for supporting social change, intercultural conversation, inquiry, and a strategic approach to conversation (205). In community literacy, university departments or faculty form centers in community settings for tutoring, writing, or other public projects in which members of both the university and community take part. In the case of the Carnegie Mellon University (CMU) Community Literacy Center, CMU students tutor high school students, mostly African American, from Pittsburgh's north side. Linda Flower (1997) situates these "community problem-solving dialogues" in the logic of "prophetic pragmatism," which has roots in the work of John Dewey but with elaboration by Cornel West (101–103). Flowers et al. (2000) offer a book-length treatment of "rival hypothesis theory" as the foundation of the intercultural inquiry at CMU's Community Literacy Center.

Another example of a community literacy center is Temple University's Institute for the Study of Literature, Literacy, and Culture, which partners with local schools, activist groups, and nonprofit organizations (such as The Poor People's Summit, an annual convention of homeless people in Philadelphia), and offers connections to Temple English department courses (Goldblatt and Parks 2000).

Teachers/Writers/Scholars in the Streets

Literacy Research and Ethnographies

Home, neighborhood, and community literacy practices have been the subject of research by many ethnographers of communication, especially those interested in new-literacy studies.[14] Qualitative researchers of literacy, such as Shirley Brice Heath, Caroline Heller, Deborah Brandt, and Brian Street, have done research that informs composition scholarship but also broadens what we consider the subjects of inquiries to include, for example, a writing group of low-income women in the Tenderloin district of San Francisco (Heller 1997). This work typically involves researchers (but not students) in projects in a neighborhood community or a small subculture, like an immigrant ladies' club (Nardini 1999). In some cases, however, researchers try to link their project sites to service-learning courses, bringing students and researchers to the same place (Cushman 2002b).

Public Writing by Academics

Peter Mortensen (1998) argues that composition scholars should seek ways to address their writing about composition to broader nonacademic audiences. Mortensen grounds his call for "going public" in questions of ethics, especially accountability to local spaces as well as national concerns. Composition teacher-researchers as public intellectuals may wish to speak about the vitality of literacy, argues Mortensen, "but they must also speak to the ethical concerns of the local—the community, the commonwealth, the region . . . . In composition, we can discharge [our public] duties by writing for the communities we live in, communities likely much larger and more complex than the institutional ones in which we work" (195). He suggests as "public duties" reviewing books for local publications and providing background or testimony for lawmakers. Ellen Cushman, in "The Public Intellectual, Service Learning and Activist Research," calls for a broader notion of public work that combines "research, teaching and service efforts in order to address social issues important to community members in under-served neighborhoods" (329). Mortensen, Cushman, and others[15] connect rhetoric and composition studies to questions about the public accountability of academics, a question raging across the disciplines and in the popular press, particularly in the writings of Michael Bérubé, Cary Nelson, bell hooks, and Stanley Fish.[16]

Community or Street Publishing

Some academics do not research local acts of communication but help facilitate and circulate them. Learner-focused community-based publishing began as a part of the international literacy movement in the late 1980s, with the goal of creating and circulating "learner produced materials" (Gayfer 1995, 3–4). In this view of community writing, publishing gives adult learners skills and relevant texts from which to practice reading and writing. This approach recalls in some ways Paulo Freire's pedagogy, wherein learners produce key words and concepts and learn to read and write through inquiries they devise and control. For Freire (1997), the purpose of such a practice is clearly political; the goal of the process is the act of *conscientization,* the developing of a critical consciousness. For the British adult, basic-writing groups that Margaret Gayfer discusses, however, the focus is on developing learners as internal audiences for texts, without explicit political goals.

Some community publishing groups do focus on external audiences, however, often with explicit political aims. "Public literacy" has become a prevalent international movement that includes the upsurge of writing groups in the United Kingdom and South Africa, where writers circulate their work publicly through self-published books and magazines. This represents intervention in public discourse by people "previously only half-seen" (Mace 1995, x). Some initiatives, such as the British Federation of Worker Writers, become "regarded as both a serious producer of writing and a significant oppositional movement" (Hayler and Thompson 1995, 41).

In the United States, academics in English composition have begun to stake out the terrain of community publishing with a public, activist focus. Temple University's Institute for the Study of Literature, Literacy, and Culture publishes *Open City*, a range of writing from local community members.[17] According to its website, the Institute believes that interdisciplinary research "within and beyond the confines of the university . . . has the potential to effect not only academic but also social change."

Another well-established community publishing project is Chicago's Neighborhood Writing Alliance, publisher of *The Journal of Ordinary Thought (JOT)*. JOT, founded by Hal Adams (a professor of education) in 1992 and currently edited by Anne Knepler (a doctoral candidate in rhetoric), works from Antonio Gramsci's notion of the organic intellectual; the back cover of every issue publishes the organization's motto: "Every Person is a Philosopher." JOT aims to cultivate and publish the voices of local writers, many living in low- and no-income areas of the city. Free writing workshops are held weekly at sites around the city, including schools, public libraries, community centers, employment centers, and homeless shelters; the journal is published quarterly. The goal of the Alliance is not to remediate writing skills but to create a serious body of literature that celebrates the artistic achievements of "ordinary" writers as well as photographers and other visual artists.[18]

Street newspapers also fall within the field of community publishing.[19] A survey that I conducted at the 2000 International Network of Street Papers conference revealed more than two dozen active writing groups for homeless and low-income writers in Europe, Africa, South America, North America, and Asia. These groups write articles and poems for publication in street papers as well as books and performance-based projects.[20]

Community publishing assists writers with what John Trimbur (2000) describes as a complex yet understudied aspect of public writing: circulation. In "Composition and the Circulation of Writing,"

Trimbur argues that circulation is a key aspect of writing that is frequently overlooked in examination of public writing and composition pedagogy. Using Marx's *Grundrisse* as a theoretical touchstone, Trimbur recommends pedagogies that include explorations of the circuits of textual circulation and authorizing, ranging from print journals to tabloids to Web discussion groups. Community publishing is one avenue that seeks to understand and create meaningful venues for circulating texts within a complex and fragmented public sphere.

Taken together, public writing, public-oriented course content, place-based writing, Web-based publishing, service learning, community literacy, ethnographies of communication, and community publishing represent a significant public turn in the field of composition. At this point, it might be useful to step back to both consider briefly how we got here and assess the value of this orientation.

Roots of the Public Turn in Composition

Pedagogical Roots of the Public Turn

Several writers have traced histories of various aspects of the public turn in composition, including service learning, public writing, and extracurricular literacy research.[21] Many of these overviews begin with work done in composition in the 1960s and 70s, but the pedagogical roots of composition's interest in public work date back to earlier years. My former History of Education professor, Gordon Brossell, worked to convince his students that most new innovations in teaching are revivals and reworkings of older practices. His claim proves true in the case of composition's public turn—or what may be more accurately termed *composition's public return*.[22] The current interest in public work does not easily trace from a single source nor through a linear genealogy, but it does draw from a diverse range of theories and past teaching practices: classical rhetoric and its many pedagogical revivals over the years; John Dewey's theories of experiential learning; Paulo Freire's theories about pedagogy as liberation; Antonio Gramsci's writings about organic intellectualism and the creation of cultural hegemony; cultural studies theories, especially from the Birmingham School that followed in the tradition of Marx and Gramsci; anthropological work and ethnographic studies of literacy within various local communities; oral history; liberation theology; philosophy geared toward the value of service; and the publishing and networking opportunities presented by the Internet.

James Berlin's "Writing Instruction in School and College English, 1890–1985" (1990) demonstrates the heterogeneity of pedagogical approaches in composition prior to the 1970s, a time that some might dismiss as the "bad old days" of current-traditional instruction. While Berlin underscores the dominance of current-traditional pedagogies and the long reach of Harvard's shadow beginning in 1892, he also notes that developing colleges and universities offered sites of ongoing challenge to the hegemony of Harvard's pedagogy (189). In the early part of the twentieth century, resistance came from Yale's liberal *belles lettres* approach to writing, and after World War I from writing teachers committed to utilitarian and vocational writing instruction. Berlin writes of such utilitarian approaches, "At its best . . . the drive for social efficiency promoted a democratic rhetoric that responded to the progressive agenda of John Dewey's full educational experience: self development within a democratic environment, a concern for social reform and harmony, and the preparation for economic integration" (194). Berlin credits several university faculty for promoting such pedagogy, including Fred Newton Scott. Scott measured the efficacy of writing by "its effect upon the welfare of the community," what Berlin calls a "rhetoric of public service" (194). Later, between the two world wars, courses inspired by Dewey and Scott that underscored "writing is a social act performed through a complex interaction of writer, audience, subject and language" could be found in every geographical region of the country (200).

After World War II, a renewed interest in classical rhetoric took place at some institutions, particularly among the Neo-Aristotelians at the University of Chicago. In the 1960s, writers such as Richard Weaver, James Murphy, and Edward P. J. Corbett helped revive a focus on rhetorical invention and the rhetorical nature of writing itself (Berlin 1990, 205).

Expressivist and cognitive pedagogies that gained prominence in the 1970s have been criticized for prioritizing personal development of student writers while ignoring social concerns.[23] While some of these critiques may be especially true of early forays in expressivism, it would be a mistake not to note the contributions to the public turn made by cognitive, expressivist, and process theorists. Janet Emig's work was groundbreaking not only for its discoveries about the recursive and knowledge-making processes inherent in writing but for its assertions about the ethical and democratic values associated with teaching writing:

> . . . [A]ll teaching possess[es] a moral dimension: teaching represents an ethical transaction with the learner, demanding responsibility, scrupulosity, and nurture . . . .
>
> . . . Indeed, we each regard the learning and teaching of composition as democratic manifestations of a democratic society requiring

serious, courteous, and equitable treatment of all persons across categories of age, gender, ethnicity, race, religion, class, sexual preference, and community status. (with Phelps, xv).

As Peter Mortensen (1998) writes, one of Emig's most radical
propositions was that composition should concern itself with studying
people (the students themselves) and not mechanisms of writing
(198). This concern with students as people with full lives beyond our
classrooms has been a hallmark of process pedagogy, which consis-
tently blurs the lines between in-school and out-of-school discourse.
Peter Elbow (1991), for example, who has written in defense of writing as personal as opposed to social, also defends the teaching of writing in broadly conceived terms because "life is long and college is
short" (136). Contemporary work in the tradition of process writing,
like Lad Tobin's work (1994), considers classroom dynamics and inter-
personal relationships among students and teachers. Tom Newkirk
(1997) asks teachers to look closely at student-chosen topics (a hallmark of the process movement) and determine what constructions of
acceptable writing we tacitly carry. While process pedagogy tends to
delimit the classroom as the salient space for examining writing, it
clearly draws from and acknowledges the implications of social
dynamics and constructions beyond the classroom.

Starting in the 1980s the boundaries for the relevant context of a
writing class broadened as concerns about writers' identity (race, class,
gender, sexual orientation, geographical location, etc.) and sociopoliti-
cal contexts for writing preoccupied people interested in composition.[24]
Critical pedagogy, feminist pedagogy, and cultural studies theory
infused composition courses with an awareness of the broad social systems and complex cultural practices that make up and inform everyday
life. Cultural studies, especially as conceived by Marxist-informed Birmingham School cultural studies figures like Stuart Hall and Dick Heb-
dige, has had significant impact on composition, influencing choices of
topics for writing, readings, and genres of writing. Ethnographic and
textual research on the nature of work, popular culture, and Supreme
Court decisions are just some of the kinds of writing gesturing to public
concerns that have been influenced by cultural studies.[25]

Beginning in the 1990s proponents of radical and feminist pedagogy
have critiqued teaching that elides questions of the political and ideological ramifications of all discourse and seek to politicize the act of teaching
and the teacher's authority.[26] Proponents of critical pedagogy encourage
students to see the systems and institutions that connect individuals and
local events. Ira Shor (1996), for example, worries that his students lack
"systematic thinking," which he describes as "a critical means to emphasize the larger social connection of single items, to locate individual situ-

ations in their larger historical contexts as part of a social system" (58). Samuel Totten notes that our information-saturated society bombards us with facts, which we experience in isolated pieces; he suggests the solution of helping students to understand and appreciate their "connectedness" to the world around them (Hurlbert and Totten 1992, 11).

Revivals of classical rhetoric and newer "epistemic" rhetoric have identified the relevant scene of writing as "a product of the interaction of the writer, the particular audience addressed, the community at large, and the subject considered" (Berlin 1990, 211). Through this construction, the community outside the classroom and its concerns become part of the relevant rhetorical situation of a writing classroom. Teacher-researchers influenced by rhetoric have focused on civic literacy and ways to help students develop as active citizens.[27] Writing courses drawing from a broadly defined rhetorical tradition range from teaching writing as an activity with social consequences to writing about social issues grounded in a classical discussion of invention.

Economic Roots of the Public Turn

The public initiatives of contemporary universities cannot solely be credited to pedagogical trends; they are powerfully driven by political agendas and a changing economic climate. Beginning in the mid-70's, a period of economic crisis and restructuring eroded the economic stability that had been built upon a decades-long compromise among manufacturers, labor unions, and governments, which David Harvey describes as the "Fordist compromise." (1989, 145) This system gave way to a post-Fordist economic system marked by revised labor arrangements, increased corporate mergers, the transfer of manufacturing to geographically peripheral locations, quick turnover of capital, increased technology, and a focus on niche marketing. A post-Fordist culture, according to Harvey, is marked by a reduction in the core of permanent salaried employees and an increasing reliance on part-time, temporary, or sub-contracted workers, resulting in widening disparities among the wealthy and disadvantaged groups, especially women and Third World workers (153). When production speeds up and becomes more flexible, the rate at which individuals consume must also accelerate in order to avoid economic crisis. According to Harvey and Paul Smith (1997), restructuring helped bring about postmodern aesthetics, fleeting fashion trends, and the marketing of rapidly advancing technologies. According to Smith, the need to "increase the modes of consumption" (xx) led to commodifying realms of experience, including education.

Economic changes have redefined how universities conceive themselves and the work they do. A college education has increasingly become marketed as brand-name experience that students purchase. What brand they buy depends on their resources and the prestige of the institution. Universities seek to create envious reputations by courting famous-name academics, pioneering high-tech research, or even connecting with local communities. This shift from a university as a site of knowledge to a prestige event grounds Bill Readings' analysis of the rhetoric of excellence and how it functions within universities (1996, 160).[28]

In the current economic climate, universities must market themselves aggressively, competing with many other institutions for tuition, government grants, alumni funding, and corporate sponsorship. Excellence functions as a form of accounting within the competitive internal environments of universities. The role and power of administration increases, mechanistic forms of evaluation are instituted, and the empty signifier of excellence is the measuring stick by which all university output is compared. And since marketing is increasingly important, administrators must continually prove their institution's value to corporations, governments, alumni, and students.

It seems no coincidence that the rise in public initiatives in universities corresponds to an increasingly competitive academic marketplace. Lillian Bridwell-Bowles (1997) argues that universities' turn toward service and public projects results from economic and political pressures to make the university seem publicly relevant (19). She connects the rise in service learning to economic changes in the 1990s that caused universities to receive greater pressure from students, parents, and legislators to have education provide "value-added," marketable skills. In 1985 the presidents of Georgetown, Brown, and Stanford have founded Campus Compact, an organization that promotes service learning, in order to counter media images of "college students as materialistic and self-absorbed." Put simply, many universities initiate community partnerships because of their own needs and interests. And like consultants who must create clients to need what they are offering, a university must develop community partnerships to fit within the university's idea of "shared or mutually compatible goals" (Adler-Kassner et al. 1997, 5). Many universities now fund outreach programs, experiential-based learning, and alternative spring breaks to act as both a draw for students and public relations for the institution.

James Berlin assesses the effect of the shift toward a post-Fordist economy on curricula in his final book, *Rhetoric, Poetics, Cultures*. Berlin argues that English department curricula must become responsive to the cultural changes of a postmodern world by training students to become communicators able to compete on the job market *and* critical citizens able to understand and respond to the changing world around them. Adjusting English curricula for a too-direct focus on training for the workforce, he argues, is difficult and risky, given the complexity and changing nature of the economy. And to attempt to do so, according to Berlin, would result in hierarchical divisions and tracking of students based on vocational choices (50). Additionally, Berlin maintains a deep belief in the democratic aims of education, which should neither slavishly serve business interests nor entirely ignore them.

Berlin's recommended approach places social-epistemic rhetoric at the heart of curricula that blur the line between literary and nonliterary, between production and consumption of texts. He recommends finding a way to place "preparation for work within a comprehensive range of democratic educational concerns," which include "situating discussions of knowledge in questions of balancing concerns for serving interests of individuals and of larger communities by helping students learn to locate the beneficiaries and victims of knowledge" (51–52). In other words, his call situates writing and English studies squarely within the public realm.

Many other scholars are responding to economic change by noting that the relevance of English curricula and college writing in the universities of the 21st century is no longer assumed. Some focus on the change toward electronic environments (Hawisher and Selfe 1999), while others argue that service to community and service learning should form the basis for the future of English departments (Cushman 2002a). All of these writers express concern about the notion of public accountability. The push is to make the study of English, of reading and writing, relevant to the world outside the university structure.

Psychological/Spiritual/Personal Roots of the Public Turn

In addition to desires for more effective pedagogy or better university public relations, the public turn in composition also involves less tangible and more personal, psychological, or spiritual concerns. Many outreach and community-service programs began as individual or student initiatives (Schutz and Gere 1998) and thrive at schools and colleges because service to others is part of the school's religious or other social mission. For some students and faculty, religious or political motivations stir their interest in local communities. At Boston College and other Jesuit universities, for example, undergraduates can choose the interdisciplinary Faith, Peace and Justice minor, for which they take classes on social issues, get involved in local communities, and write a thesis that combines research and analysis of a social problem through an ethical lens developed from liberation theology or some other social-religious theory.

Many writers have suggested that their interests in public or extracurricular writing and service learning stem from their need for more hope and optimism for themselves and their students in a world of drastic economic inequity and political upheaval. Some describe this need as a desire to counteract "student alienation and despair" (Dorman and Dorman 1997); others, to help students feel like "more effective participants in public life" (Cooper and Julier 1997); still others wish to learn ways for acting in a "fragmented" world dominated by "a culture of disconnect" (George 2002). This desire to be a connected agent in the world, active in ways other than as a consumer (see Mathieu 1999), is a healthy hope, one shared by many faculty and students. Teachers often work long hours for little pay. In order to get up in the morning and work under material conditions that for many are less than ideal, we seek to overcome feelings of cynicism about our ability to be relevant in the world and embrace some form of optimism. And for many teachers, public writing has become that source. In other words, in a world (and within institutions) that are increasingly complex, corporately managed and alienating, we all need some good news, something to give us hope. Some have found that hope by connecting with local initiatives in the community.

Spatial and Temporal Politics and the Sites of Pedagogy

Often-conflicted economic, pedagogical, and personal agendas have brought street issues into the classroom and classroom practices out into the streets. But whatever the reasons, the public turn in composition is more than just a pedagogical option. It represents a significant redrawing of geographic boundaries that define sites for composition teaching and research. Redrawing the terrain thus requires rethinking our terms for designing and evaluating successful work.

Scholarship in composition is paying increased attention to the spaces within which teaching and research take place. From pedagogical theory that argues attentiveness to spatial politics to pedagogies that attend to the specificity and importance of place, composition has become increasingly attentive to the rhetorical and material power of places. In an issue of *Symploke* devoted to "The Sites of Pedagogy," Jeffrey Di Leo, Walter Jacobs, and Amy Lee argue that "pedagogical theory premised upon the classroom as a constant is no longer acceptable . . . We must learn how to adjust our pedagogy to account for the changing nature of the classroom" (8). Pedagogy, they argue, must be attentive to individual "sites of pedagogy," which they define as "the locations of pedagogical address," the "spaces in which interactions between teacher and student occur" (7). Di Leo, Jacobs, and Lee (2002) encourage a radical rethinking of pedagogy in light of the new pedagogical sites brought about by outreach initiatives, technology, and the changing economy: "While it may be obvious that pedagogical processes are affected by the setting in which they occur, we understand far too little about this relationship to be able to maximize its learning potential. Gaining a better understanding of the sites in which we teach and learn is critical to improving education" (7).

Nedra Reynolds (1998) similarly recommends that scholars of composition should confront many of our tacit assumptions about place and space. She examines how imaginary geographies prevail within composition scholarship, including metaphorical configurations such as community and city. She instead encourages a more active "politics of space"—an explicit examination of the relationship between material conditions and imagined territories. "A spatial politics of writing, " she writes, "works to deny transparent space and to attend to neglected places in their material reality rather than their imaginary forms" (30). Reynolds (2004) sees the study and awareness of place as central to outreach initiatives that send students into street communities: "Along with sending students to communities that surround and support the university, we also need to encourage their understanding of the politics of space in the immediate university environment" (136).

What this scholarship encourages is a place-sensitive awareness of our teaching and scholarship. Academic work that has traditionally taken place only within institutional boundaries is now crossing borders more frequently and blurring the lines delineating university and community. At the same time, however, most of the means for designing, launching, and evaluating street initiatives originate within universities and continue to rely on institutional logics or student outcomes for evaluating teaching or research. The fierce competition within institutions for resources has helped promote uncritical rhetoric about public initiatives. Isaacs and Jackson (2001) argue that in "writing for the 'real world,' service learning and web-based instruction— public writing has been embraced seemingly without question" (xvi). They argue that questions of ethics are often elided or ignored. Even though composition theory continues to increase its critical awareness and theoretical sophistication regarding outreach initiatives,[29] fuller attention to the motivations, consequences, and assumptions governing turns to the street is warranted. Our scholarship has not fully considered how to design and assess street initiatives in ways that attend to the specificities of individual places, people, and times. Understanding specificities of time and place, especially institutional spaces, is fruitfully explored in the work of Michel de Certeau.

On Tactics and Hope

Michel de Certeau on Tactics

In *Practice of Everyday Life*, Michel de Certeau categorizes ways of operating in the world based on one's relationship to institutional spaces, and in doing so, makes a distinction between *strategies* and *tactics*. He describes *strategies* as calculated actions that emanate from and depend upon "proper" (as in propertied) spaces, like corporations, state agencies, and educational institutions, and relate to others via this proper space: "A strategy assumes a place that can be circumscribed as *proper (propre)* and thus serve as the basis for generating relations with an exterior distinct from it (competitors, adversaries, 'clienteles,' 'targets' or 'objects' of research)" (xx). The goal of a strategy is to create a stable, spatial nexus that allows for the definition of practices and knowledge that minimize temporal uncertainty. Strategic thinking accounts for and relies on measurability and rationality.

On the other hand, *tactics*, according to de Certeau, are at one's disposal when one "cannot count on a 'proper' (a spatial or institutional location, nor thus on a borderline distinguishing the other as a visble totality)" (xx). Tactics are available when we do not control the space:

> The place of a tactic belongs to the other. A tactic insinuates itself into the other's place, fragmentarily, without taking it over in its entirety, without being able to keep it at a distance. It has at its disposal no base where it can capitalize on its advantages, prepare its expansions, and secure independence with respect to circumstances. The "proper" is a victory of place over time. On the contrary, since it does not have a place, a tactic depends on time—it is always on the watch for opportunities that must be seized "on the wing." (xx)

To act tactically means to "take advantage of 'opportunities' and depend upon them" (37). Rhetorical theory, not scientific discourse, according to de Certeau, allows for an exploration into and an understanding of tactics. He lists the Sophists, Sun Tzu's *The Art of War,* and the Arabic anthology *The Book of Tricks* as important examples of rhetoric as tactical art, a "tradition of a logic articulated on situations and the will of others" (xx).

Universities are organized by strategies: academic calendars, disciplinary rules and methods of assessment, and organization along strategic units, such as colleges, departments, and institutes. When extending university work into the community, existing academic measures are often applied—such as grading criteria, methods for evaluation, desires for institutionalization—even though the space of the interaction is no longer defined or controlled by the university. For example, evaluation of service learning relies mostly on student performance and satisfaction, standard measures of academic work.[30] To apply strategic rules calls upon a potentially colonizing logic that seeks to control the space of the interaction through stability and long-term planning. My argument is that when moving from the classroom into the streets, scholars, teachers, and writers must devise new time- and space-appropriate methods for how we plan and evaluate our work. Thinking strategically, then, is not an option, because the dynamic spaces where we work should not be considered strategic extensions of academic institutions.

Tactics seek rhetorically timely actions, as de Certeau asserts: "strategies pin their hopes on the resistance that the *establishment of a place* offers to the erosion of time; tactics on a clever *utilization of time*, of the opportunities it presents and also of the play that it introduces into the foundations of power" (38–39). If one applies tactical logic to community-based university work, one seeks not stability but clever uses of time. Also, tactical measures of success are grounded not in scientific proof but in rhetorical—and thus changeable—ideas and arguments. Tactics foreground the temporal and spatial challenges that street-based projects must always face—time challenges, incompatible schedules, the often conflicted spatial politics involved in deciding on whose turf work can and should take place.[31] Seeing community work as tactical helps teachers and students realistically assess what work is possible and be open to radically redefining what is desirable academic-community work. Such an orientation requires a critical spirit of inquiry, based not on certainty but on hope. I focus on *hope* as the concept that best describes the spirit of tactical relationships.

Ernst Bloch on Hope

Hope is a word that gets tossed around loosely in today's world, and is often used synonymously with *wishing*. For example, "I hope that _____ (fill in an ideal man or woman) calls me," is not a hope at all, but a wish. There is little the speaker can do to bring about or prevent the call. Hope in its deepest philosophical and political meanings invokes something quite different than wishing. To take on hope is to take on risk and responsibility while maintaining a dogged optimism.

The most fully conceived treatment of hope can be found in the work of the Marxist utopian philosopher Ernst Bloch. His three-volume *Principles of Hope* was written in the U.S. between 1938 and 1947; it was published in German in 1959 and translated into English in 1986. Bloch has been called "the political philosopher of hope" (Zipes 1997, 1). His extensive and ideosyncratic writing on utopia and hope has won him both admirers and critics. Yet for many years his work was largely discredited or overlooked because of his idealism or because of the ways he himself lived or failed to live out his political views:

> [Many] German intellectuals have turned away from Bloch because of his compromising relations with the East German government. Or, they have rejected Bloch because of his idealism: how can one speak about hope and utopia when millions of people are unemployed in Germany and when violent xenophobia has erupted, not only in Germany, but through most of Europe? . . . [I]n the United States and Great Britain, Bloch has never really been taken all that seriously anyway. (Zipes, 1)[32]

At a time in history when many have declared Marxism dead and Marxist theory irrelevant, Ernst Bloch has recently received renewed critical attention[33] precisely because his work on utopia and hope, which may seem terribly out of time, asserts exactly what many need right now: "a stubborn hope for a better life" (Daniel and Moylan 1997, vii); "militant optimism" (Levitas 1997, 70); and "the capacity to imagine the totality as something completely different" (Daniel and Moylan, viii). Bloch's English translator, Jack Zipes (1997), describes Bloch's importance this way:

> Against despair and against fashionable postmodernist thinking, Bloch's philosophy of hope provides a sober perspective for, and useful categories to grasp and move out of, the dark morass of present-day politics. Moreover, many of his philosophical principles can provide an important impetus in radical cultural work, even as they need to be elaborated and applied in concrete situations. (3)

Bloch's ideal of hope can offer a conceptual tool for teachers that allows us to critically interrogate the limitations of university-community partnerships while also understanding their tactical possibilities, to look at the current moment with an eye toward a better future. To Bloch, hope is a critical utopian articulation of a "future anticipated."[34] His idealistic vision of Marxism combines critical reflection with action. According to Ze'ev Levy (1997), Bloch views the world optimistically, as a "laboratory of possible good (*laboratorium possibilis salutis*) something that has not yet been completely realized" (175).

In order to move from the category of possibility to reality, according to Bloch, one must see utopia not as an abstraction or an idealized blueprint but as a continually open vision toward which one keeps working. Hope is a gesture that seeks to move out of abstractions about a better world toward actions devised to change the current world. Bloch (1986) writes that one should not understand hope only as "emotion . . . but more essentially as a directing act of a cognitive kind" (I:12). In this sense, hope embodies three important components: emotional desire or longing, cognitive reflection or analysis, and action. To hope is not merely to wish but to combine wishful thinking with willful thinking and willful action (see Levitas 1997, 67). "Educated hope" exercises a constant dialectic between reason and passion (Levitas, 68): "Educated hope, *docta spes,* is born out of and articulates [a] relationship between end and means, passion and reason, aspiration and possibility. It represents the transformation of wishful thinking into wish-full and effective acting, the move from the dream to the dream come true" (Levitas, 73).

Defined in these terms, hope is more active and critical than a wish. We must realize what our world—or community partnerships— is missing and acknowledge what our work cannot achieve, in order to hope and work for a better future. Bloch worries that if people become too consumed with the present, they risk losing the ability to imagine a radically other future: the *novum*—the unexpectedly new, which pushes humanity toward a not-yet-realized future. To Bloch (and other cultural critics, like Herbert Marcuse), the positive of utopia derives from the negative, from an awareness of "the radical insufficiency of the present" (Moylan 1986, 22). Hope is what mediates between the insufficient present and an imagined but better future.

To acknowledge the present as radically insufficient is a hopeful action, when acting as a prerequisite for future actions and imaginings. To see the present as insufficient does not imply that one passively accepts it as such. Nor does it mean that one closes one's eyes, fantasizes, and merely wishes for a better world. Bloch (1988) writes that hope is "the opposite of security. It is the opposite of naïve optimism. The category of danger is always within it . . . . Hope is not confidence. If it could not be disappointed, it would not be hope . . . . Thus, hope is critical and can be disappointed" (16–17).

To hope, then, is to look critically at one's present condition, assess what is missing, and then long for and work for a not-yet reality, a future anticipated. It is grounded in imaginative acts and projects, including art and writing, as vehicles for invoking a better future.

When working in local streets and neighborhoods, a commitment of hope allows for the kind of motivation and affirmation that tactical work requires, which means admitting failures, seeing one's work as insufficient, and recognizing that success to some constituents might look different to others. To embrace hope is not to feel personally defeated when projects don't work perfectly; but it is also a commitment not to be complacent or accepting of problems. Hope is the tension between reality and vision that provides the energy and motivation to keep working. In order to establish credibility with the people in the streets where we work, we need to conduct our work with humility and a critical eye. A utopian theory of hope allows for that orientation. The perpetual challenge of hope is the need to keep our work open, changing, and continually evolving. This need stands in opposition to desires for our research to offer clear methodologies and data, create long-term projects, make permanent change.

Tactics of Hope

Tactical work grounded in hope encourages teachers, writers, and scholars to continually seek new ways to listen to the community around them, to acknowledge what isn't working or isn't possible—not as a way to "troubleshoot" but to combine passion, analysis, and action in order to keep working toward a better future. *Tactics of hope* encourage an orientation of frank questioning of the ethically troubling aspects of work in the streets. Starting with "Why are we here?"[35] we can ask even deeper questions: Are there better things to be doing now? Is our work welcomed? And who do we need to ask, and how, in order to decide?

Chris Gallagher in *Radical Departures* defines pedagogy not as theory to be applied but a process that must be forged communally. This claim is especially true when pedagogy extends into the streets. Our scholarship does a good job of spelling out tenets and guidelines for street work. The difficulty lies in *how* to move from calls for reciprocity, public action, and self-reflexivity toward specific ways of acting and imagining concrete visions in local times and places. No template can be devised; public work is "local, messy and complex" (Schutz and Gere 1998, 185). Rather, deeply questioning the processes of public writing, street issues in the classroom, students in the streets, and teachers in the streets— from the perspectives of those we purportedly serve—is one way to begin listening and learning to answer these questions.

Tactics of hope suggests a conceptual framework for imagining and evaluating university-neighborhood connections that are responsive, open, and changing as conditions in the streets or neighborhoods change. *Tactics of hope* is meant to raise questions about the public turn in composition, not to condemn the good and important work that is being done nor to advance one intellectual position over another in an academic quarrel. Seeing our work as hopeful and tactical is meant to affirm the ethical and grounded work that so many teachers and students are doing every day, by outlining issues and questions that may help our work become more responsive to those in the streets. Again, this is not a desire to ruin or dampen success stories of community work but to redefine what we consider a "success story" to be. Long-term success for public-oriented composition work depends not on controlling community spaces but in devising timely and spatially appropriate relationships in the streets where we work. In order to be rhetorically responsive, we need to learn how to attend to people and places, which means asking, listening, and learning. I suggest several categories for the kinds of questions to be asking here—questions of time, space, credibility, knowledge, and success:

Questions of Time

- How much time are we willing to invest to learn about local issues and local spaces?
- How can we better understand the timeliness (or *kairos*) of public issues or projects that we bring into our classes and plan our teaching accordingly?
- Can we define projects that are worthwhile for those in the streets in the time we do have?
- Can we translate the artificiality of the academic calendar into useful and meaningful rhythms for those not familiar with this schedule? Can we define projects that meet local needs within this strangely configured time?
- How does time affect our work: Is a worthwhile research or service-learning project this semester going to be useful or necessary next semester or next year?

Questions of Space

- How can we define projects that stay attuned to the fact that spaces on the streets are never static, that needs within non-profits and neighborhoods continually change?
- What are the institutions that define conditions in a given local setting? How many of them are local and how many extend far beyond this neighborhood?
- How do issues or pieces of literature from the street change when they are brought into the university classroom?
- What rhetorical spaces do acts of public writing inhabit? What must writing look like to create an audience in that space?

Questions of Credibility

- How well known or respected are we in the streets where we work?
- How valuable do the agencies and neighborhoods we work with find our work?
- How can we commit ourselves to work and to listen in ways that will help us improve our long-term credibility with local groups?

- How can teachers represent the intellectual work or the struggles of a group of which we are not a member?
- How can we improve ourselves as public writers and publishers who are recognized within some public spheres?

Questions of Knowledge

- What do we need to know about a specific street or neighborhood before we start connecting our teaching, writing, or research there?
- How can we learn ways to listen and ask questions that bring more than silence?
- How can we cultivate new skills and projects that are of use to the public?
- What do we need to know as writers in order to teach public writing better?

Questions of Success

- How do we determine the success or failure of our public acts—writing and service?
- How can we seek more response from the streets in evaluating our work?
- How can we seriously examine the pitfalls of our projects without losing hope?

The following chapters take up these questions, in terms of the various movements of composition's public turn that I have outlined here: writing in the streets, street life in the classroom, students in the streets, and finally teachers/writers/scholars in the streets. This book offers one tactical gesture to share some voices of those in the streets who accommodate, become involved with, and with any luck, benefit from our publicly oriented courses.

Notes

1. I do not mean to suggest that the "public turn" describes a movement of the entire field of composition studies. Rather, composition has become an increasingly heterogenous field with initiatives and scholarship that specialize in an array of literacy issues, such as academic writing, EFS, writing across the curriculum, technology and writing, etc. A public turn represents just one significant development of composition studies, an elaboration and articulation of composition's *social turn* (see Weisser for an overview).

2. E.g., Wells; Clark; Heilker.

3. E.g., George, 2003; Hurlbert and Totten; Owens; Mack.

4. E.g., Adler Kassner et al.; (1999; 2002a, 2002b); Deans (2000a; 2000b); or the service-learning journal *Reflections*.

5. See Farmer, Cushman, and Flower (1997, 2003).

6. See Chapter 2 for more on public writing.

7. See Sosnoski, Harkin, and Feldman; Blitz et al.; Pagnucci and Mauriello.

8. There are too many to name, but see Ford and Schave; Feldman, Downs, and McManus; Muth; George and Trimbur; Verburg.

9. For cultural studies English courses, see Berlin and Vivion; Pentikoff and Brodkey. For rhetoric of cultural studies classes, see Downing and Sosnoski; Mathieu and Sosnoski. See also Mathieu, Sosnsoski, and Zauhar; McComiskey.

10. See Dobrin and Weisser; Owens.

11. See Derek Owen's 21st Century Neighborhood Project at http://www.ourmap.org and the Boston College place-writing project at http://www.bc.edu/fws. See also Mathieu et al.

12. See McComiskey and Ryan; Reynolds (1998; 2004); Di Leo et al.

13. See Peck et al.; Goldblatt and Parks; Brandt.

14. See Hull and Schultz for a useful overview.

15. See Gallagher; Farmer; Schiappa.

16. For Fish on public intellectualism, see Weisser. For more on this, see Chapter 5.

17. See Goldblatt and Parks, and http://www.temple.edu/isllc/ncp/index.html.

18. See http://www.jot.org.

19. See Chapter 2 as well as Mathieu 2003 and Mathieu et al. 2004.

20. In Graz, Austria, *Megaphon* runs a writing group composed of African refugees. The group has produced a collection of essays on dislocation and relocation that are combined with work by Austrian citizens, to make common cause of the issues of dislocation (Schmied).

21. See Deans (2002b) and Julier for service learning. See Weisser; Isaacs and Jackson for public writing. See Hull and Schultz for new literacy research.

22. I thank Stuart Brown for this phrase, which he used at the 2004 CCCC Research Network Forum.

23. See Tobin for an insider's critique of process pedagogy. For a more detailed discussion of social construction in composition during the early 1980s, see Weisser 20–21.

24. E.g., Malinowitz; Gilyard; Villanueva.

25. Cf. Note 9.

26. See Weisser 26–27.

27. See Eberly; Heilker; Ervin; Clark; Mathieu 1999; Crowley and Hawhee.

28. See Downing, Hurlbert, and Mathieu on corporatization and English studies.

29. See Chapter 4.

30. E.g., Duffy; Kendrick and Suarez.

31. For spatial struggles related to service, see Chaden et al.

32 While not seeking to pass judgment on Bloch's political actions, I think it is important to mention them, to allow his critical work to reverberate with all of its contradictions.

33. See Daniel and Moylan.

34. Elsewhere, I have written about utopian theory's relevance for evaluating our teaching in community settings (Mathieu 2003). I describe Paulo Freire's indebtedness to utopia and a politics of hope, as well as a similar brand of militant optimism found in feminist theory, especially in feminist critical utopias.

35. This is an important question articulated by Lorie Goodman as well as Linda Flower (1997).

Two

Writing in the Streets[1]

We can never predict the impact of our actions . . . But we need to believe that our individual involvement is worthwhile, that what we do in the public sphere will not be in vain.

—Paul Loeb

Writing as Auto Insurance

What does writing *do*? In a performative sense, what does any act of writing accomplish in the world—either practically, personally, or politically? This may be the most basic yet difficult question a writer or writing teacher asks.

A traditional view of writing instruction measures the relevance and efficacy of writing within institutional boundaries and frameworks: The purpose of writing instruction is to bestow skills that prepare students for the next class or writing challenge; the audience of student writing is usually the individual instructor or the academic community that the instructor represents. Within this logic, writing functions as a form of cultural capital and writing classes (and by extension a college degree) operate transactionally, by bestowing on students institutional accreditation that they will cash in, so to speak, in future classes or at graduation. The value of a writing class thus conceived lies at least partially beyond itself. The purpose and audiences of any writing assignment are incidental, because the payoff of a course lies more in its grade and in the rehearsal of writing conventions than through any events or projects that transpire within the class itself.

Many composition scholars oppose defining the parameters of a writing course in strictly institutional terms. Geoffrey Sirc (2002), for example, critiques an orientation that he calls "Freshman English as Corporate Seminar," which he describes as writing courses that privilege preparation for work over "intensification of experience" (8–9). Patricia Harkin (2002) characterizes the institutional function of freshman writing as the university equivalent of automobile insurance—it's something no student ever wants to purchase, but they do it anyhow . . . just in case they "need" it at some future moment. As the corporate seminar and auto insurance metaphors connote, viewing writing as a universal requirement that exists only to transact skills or status limits the purview of writing and writing classes to the institutional setting. While few would contest the value of equipping students with writing skills and conventions that will serve them throughout their academic and work careers, many writing instructors also seek a variety of pedagogical approaches that move beyond narrow institutional definitions of writing.[2] One of these pedagogical responses has been inviting students to engage in public writing, which many feel gives students more intrinsic motivations for their writing by seeing broader purposes or audiences for their work.[3]

In some classrooms, public writing might mean sharing work among students through peer workshops, collaborative work, or classroom circulation of finished works. In others, public writing means asking that students' work involve the streets, by gearing writing toward public purposes and extracurricular audiences. In these courses, writing may become less like auto insurance, but what does it becomes more like? When the purview of a writing class encompasses issues and concerns in the streets, what can public writing accomplish? And how do we know?

Scholars such as Susan Wells, Rosa Eberly, John Trimbur, and Christian Weisser have explored the myriad complications and challenges associated with asking students to write and circulate texts publicly, including the limitations on a classroom to become a public space (Eberly); a lack of a clear, unified public sphere to which one can appeal (Wells); a need to consider complex motivations for public writing and means of circulating public texts (Trimbur); and a need to understand the range of complex theories about public spheres (Weisser). Additionally, contributors to *Public Works* (Isaacs and Jackson, 2001) raise questions about the risks, limits, and losses that can accompany a turn toward public writing. In short, while many in composition are drawn to the immediate rhetorical situations that public writing offers, the consequences of such a turn are multiple, complex, and not easy to summarize.

Weisser (2002) describes composition's growing interest in public writing as a "logical and progressive development of the field" (90). He notes that while many writing teachers have turned to public writing in order to give student writing greater significance, he worries that "few compositionists know where 'the public' is located, and even fewer have thought in depth about what public writing might entail beyond letters to the editor of a newspaper or to their local congressman" (92). Eberly (1999) writes that "because writing classrooms are in many senses prefab—the group has come together for institutional more than overtly political purposes," the writing classroom can never itself become a public sphere but rather a "protopublic sphere," a place where students can explore and write for various audiences (172). For Weisser, a more refined understanding of the functioning of public spheres "in context" is necessary for theorists and teachers interested in public writing. This entails exploring the political, historical, and ideological frameworks creating and limiting public sphere participation and individuals' access to it. Borrowing from Nancy Fraser and Susan Wells, Weisser recommends that public writing in classrooms should help students discover various "counterpublics" where writers may find receptive audiences.

The implication of Weisser's argument is that one must learn about public writing by immersing oneself in it, as it occurs on the streets: "Perhaps the best way to conceptualize [a historical notion of public writing] is to examine the sites in which public writing occurs" (95). Diana George (2002) similarly writes about the need for composition scholars to first become more intimately acquainted with publications and writers seeking to raise public issues. She writes that composition scholars "have only begun to investigate" how public writing "works itself out beyond the walls of our classrooms" (6). She encourages academics to investigate how public writing functions in specific times and venues, especially by paying closer attention to small publications and advocacy groups. George claims that there is much to learn from those already writing in the streets, especially where and how to imagine purposes and audiences for public writing. "Perhaps in the end," she writes, "it is finding out where to begin that is left out in most of our talk of public writing. And, it is in reading the extraordinary words of ordinary men and women writing for local, little known causes, that we might just discover where to begin" (16).

This chapter takes up the recommendations of Weisser and George to explore local instances of public writing in the streets. In it, I describe the work of one Chicago activist/writer, a writing group I ran for three years in Chicago with low-income and homeless writers, and a Seattle street newspaper assessing the impact of their first ten years of publishing. Through these stories, I relay some lessons those in the streets can offer to writing teachers who want to explore public writing in the classroom. In short, I have learned that public writing by non-mainstream groups relies primarily on tactical rather than strategic power. This means that each act of writing contributes to ongoing campaigns, which operate through series of temporary interventions, with clear purposes but often without certain goals; conclusions and assessments are discovered only in the long-term. To engage in tactical writing requires ongoing engagement with specific issues, a long-term vision, and a critical understanding of hope—all of which can be difficult to include in a single academic semester.

In the previous chapter, I explored tactics of hope as a configuration potentially useful for helping teachers and students orient their work with local communities. As I explore public writing in various street locations through the lens of tactics of hope in this chapter, I suggest ways to adapt tactical understandings of public writing to classrooms. By exploring and taking part in the public works of activists and writers in the streets, teachers and students of composition have much to learn about and contribute to public discourse.

Jesus Christ Froze to Death

C. is an activist in Chicago who has worked for several years on campaigns to make utilities more affordable for the poor and elderly of Illinois. I talked with C. about the role writing plays in his work and how he makes a public impact on an issue. "I have to write the same message month after month," he said. "But I have to say it in different ways and to different people. I need to make an ongoing reality seem urgent" (2003). He sees his task as raising the public profile of an issue that many don't think about and making it seem timely. He must appeal to many audiences, including city and state officials, utilities executives, news reporters, Illinois voters, and most importantly the poor and elderly directly affected by utility rates. His job is a matter of life and death, he says, citing the increasing numbers of Chicago-area deaths related to lack of heat or cooling coupled with brutal winters and scorching summers. When lobbying for the winter heating programs ends, the push for summer cooling funding immediately begins. The need is ongoing. His job is both practical and visionary—helping clients fill out forms for existing aid and lobbying in public ways for funding that doesn't yet exist. How does C. manage to say the same thing over again in different ways? "I'm possessed," he explains. "A lot of creativity is coming out of me—poems, stories, film ideas, but all around this issue."

C. characterizes the public writing he does as "continually trying to start fires," creating and recreating new projects, performances, and happenings that *might* make people take notice. Sometimes the need is to write informational brochures to help clients claim the limited services that do exist. At other times, he must create a public stir, raise eyebrows, and try to interest reporters or government officials in the seemingly banal issue of utility prices. This kind of writing takes on various forms (poems, newsletters, press releases, songs) and is frequently coupled with some type of symbolic action, such as hunger strikes, rallies, and public art events. The group C. works with seeks to create unusual and provocative texts that gain attention in short bursts and to keep the bursts occurring time and time again. One year at Christmastime, for example, C. created a holiday card/poem that was distributed to lawmakers, local press, and elders in public housing. Entitled "Jesus Christ Froze to Death," the poem, printed in Spanish and English, evokes the iconic image of the baby Jesus, but instead of placing him in a manger, C. writes of Jesus "in a very cold water flat" with the 100,000 other Chicago residents whose heat had been turned off during the winter months. Angry in tone, the poem ends with the benediction, "Blessed be justice for all/Bendita sea la justicia para todos." Simultaneously reverent and irreverent, this act of public writing mixes the call for justice with invocations of Christianity, blatantly criticizes the state of public welfare.

Several months later, the summer cooling program campaign organized a public rally in support of proposed legislation to guarantee low-income elders affordable gas and electric costs. C. wrote a press release with the provocative headline "How do you like your elders? Baked? Boiled? Or Fried?" Here C. jarringly combined a deliberate act of honorific naming (according to C., "elders" is an important term because it implies honored and valued members of a community, while also invoking religious discourse) with dark humor. The goal of the press release was to garner attention for the public event, which combined a public rally with storytelling and performance. He described the day as follows: "We took one block of the city and covered it entirely with fabric squares; on each square was painted the name of each of the 700-plus elders who have died in Chicago since 1995 of what the city is calling 'heat-related deaths.' We call it 'lack of electricity shock.'" By physically filling the city space with the names of more than 700 people who died preventable deaths, the campaigners gave the numbers and the issue a verbal, visual, and human presence. The embodied presence of young people and elders who had engaged in a hunger strike together also lent physical embodiment to the event.

I talked to C. on the same night the rally had taken place. He sounded tired but enthusiastic. "We won," he said. When I asked him what he meant by winning, he said that the state announced the availability of summer cooling funds on the same day of the rally, July 1. "Last year, the funding wasn't released until August 15," he said, "and the winter program begins on September 1. That means people had to sweat out the summer with no relief and only had two weeks to apply for the cooling funds." There is no way to determine whether the rally directly caused the early announcement; governments rarely credit pressure groups for prompting their decisions. And while this victory is important to the lives of many elders, the gains are temporary. The writing and lobbying remains ongoing. This rally was important as one in a series of events. As C. explained that night, "We're distributing 15,000 fliers a month; this month we should have a newsletter that will make our presence consistent."

The kind of public writing that C. describes involves intentional acts of naming, rhetorical word play, shock value, inventive design, street theater, and parody—all are tactics to bring issues to the public consciousness. No single act of writing is ever final or determinative. Public writing, in C.'s work and the work of many activists, is about creating an ongoing discourse around an issue and working to keep that idea in the public's mind. It is a matter of many projects and actions over a sustained period of time, with different audiences and desired goals. Sometimes, C. admits, the secondary audiences are more important than the primary ones. For example, to gain the trust and commitment of the elders, the organization must be seen speaking out and taking action critical to the government. Here public writing is about connecting with people, making them feel represented and encouraging them to get involved.

When I asked C. if and how he assesses the success of public writing, he said that it's hard to evaluate a single press release, event, or newsletter. When working to set fires, "you never know which one is going to catch." He said that, in general, he knows if the work is on target based on the responses he gets from the low-income and elderly constituents he works with—whether they show up at meetings, take part in rallies, help out in the office. "We have a meeting and describe the next campaign, then we pass the hat. We always get the money we need—I can be sure that we wouldn't get it if we were off target." More importantly, C. said, their recent campaign evoked a surge of stories about power shutoffs from all over the state. The campaign set up an answering machine to provide callers with a "hotline" for information.

When I called, the message began as follows: "We refuse to sit by as our elders die unnecessary heat-related deaths and 52,000 households in our state are without power." The message then gave detailed information about an upcoming rally, including where buses would depart and numerous ways callers could participate, including signing up to follow utility-company vehicles in sound trucks warning neighbors of pending shutoffs, or calling the governor to support a cooling program. This kind of information offers callers a glimpse of the various "fires being set" and lists many ways to get involved.

Over time, however, something unexpected has happened with the hotline. Rather than just receiving information, callers have been talking back, telling their own stories of shutoffs. One call came from a U.S. soldier who returned home from Iraq to find his family's utilities cut off. "Hearing how people express on the phone is so powerful and effective when they tell their stories," C. said. "It helps us know we're on target." The campaign began archiving the messages (53 at last count) and is creating a video, using the recorded phone testimonials as the audio track.

Public Writing as Tactical

The public projects of C. and his collaborators differ from typical classroom writing assignments in various ways; C.'s campaigns focus on specific issues in ongoing ways that change in content and form as the time and audience dictates. Public audiences are often unreceptive or difficult to move; clear measures of success or completion are difficult to find. In her scholarship on public writing, Susan Wells (1996) explores the challenge of creating clear audiences and purposes: "Our public sphere is attenuated, fragmented, and colonized: so is everyone else's. All speakers who aspire to intervene in society face the task of constructing a responsive public" (328–329). Following Jurgen Habermas' *Structural Transformation of the Public Sphere*, Wells describes public discourse not as a type or genre of writing, but as "a complex array of discursive practices, including forms of writing, speech, and media performance" in which speakers and writers "come to the public with a weight of personal and social experience . . . [and] render those experiences intelligible to any listener" (328). Similarly, C. and his colleagues seek creative ways to engage the commitment and support of low-income residents and to gain the attention of state agencies and the press.

Without the power of state agencies to command media attention, activist groups face additional difficulties when trying to gain access to the public sphere. Oscar Negt and Alexander Kluge's *The Public Sphere and Experience* (1993) disputes Habermas' idea that the public sphere is open to all. They describe the public sphere as aligned with the ruling classes and institutions, which stands in contrast to what they call "proletarian experience." At the same time, though, Negt and Kluge argue that excluded groups cannot simply disconnect from this public sphere: "If the masses try to fight a ruling class reinforced by the power of the public sphere, their struggle is hopeless; they are always simultaneously fighting against themselves, for the public sphere is constituted by them" (xlvii).[4] Wells discusses Negt and Kluge in her discussion of public writing, claiming that "allusively . . . they suggest tactics for creating partial, temporary, and multiple public spheres" (334). This notion of tactical alternatives—multiple publics and counterpublics—is fruitfully pursued in the work of Michel de Certeau.

As I described in Chapter 1, de Certeau's work acknowledges both agency and limitations in his distinction between strategic and tactical power, an idea he extends to discourse as well. Strategic discourses, as he describes them, are official, emanating from institutions, media conglomerates, and state agencies. In the lives of the elders and C.'s community group, strategic discourses include utility policies, gas bills, application forms for state assistance, housing policy regulations, welfare, and Medicaid rules. They also include commonplace beliefs about poverty and the responsibility of individuals or state agencies to provide financial assistance (Stark 1992). Since strategic discourses emanate (or are circulated) from secured institutional spaces, according to de Certeau, their power is spatial and relatively stable.

Tactical discourses, on the other hand, are "determined by the absence of power" (de Certeau 1984, 38) and are calculated actions emanating from unofficial places that lack a propertied locus. Since this discourse is not issued systematically from a proper space, tactical discourse operates "within enemy territory" and without "the option of planning a general strategy." Thus tactical actions operate as "isolated actions, blow by blow" (37). They are located temporally (and temporarily), not spatially. Tactical discourse includes trickery, polemics, and tales of miracles. For example, de Certeau discusses how the Brazilian peasants of Pernambuco talk about their situation (15–18). He sees their discourse as operating on two levels: the polemical level which acknowledges their lack of institutional power—"they always fuck us over" (16)—and a utopian level of play and possibilities, filled in this case with stories of miracles centered around Frei Damião. These miracle stories respond to the socioeconomic situation from the outside "with irrelevance and impertinence" in a discourse that one cannot prove, but must only believe. These utopian stories according to de Certeau, exist as another discourse alongside the analysis of facts, "as the equivalent of what a political ideology introduces into that analysis" (17).

The power of tactical discourse, since it responds to strategic power without a stable spatial nexus, is temporary and fleeting. The effects of tactical discourse are not easily measurable in the short term and their overall effects are not always clear.

At times, C.'s group works with elders to claim the available strategic resources—funding proposals, vouchers for utility-debt relief. At other times, the group seeks to change the terms of strategic power through public, tactical campaigns.

To further explore public writing as tactical, I turn to a few stories from a writing group I ran at a Chicago street newspaper for two and a half years.

The *StreetWise* Writers Group

As I mention in the Introduction, street papers operate in urban centers worldwide with a goal of providing income and a public voice to people who are homeless or at risk of becoming homeless. Low-income or homeless people sell street papers in cities to the reading public; the papers typically include an editorial focus on homelessness and poverty-related issues. Since 1992, Chicago's *StreetWise* has regularly published articles, columns, and poetry by the men and women who sell the paper as a means of income. When I became a volunteer copy editor there in 1997, any vendor wanting to write for the paper had to do so without support from the thinly stretched editorial staff. In my job as copy editor, I regularly typed and edited articles handwritten and turned in by vendors. If I couldn't read the writing or if useful information was missing, questions remained unanswered unless the writer happened to stop in the editorial office. I edited stories using best guesses that often weren't very good. Editorial changes were explained to writers only in chance encounters. Some writers were understandably angry or hurt because they felt their ideas had been changed. I suggested setting up a group for interested writers, one that would engage them in the entire writing process, where changes to the work would be made *with* them. The newspaper's editor asked if I would run the group, and I agreed.

The weekly writing group began meeting on a snowy Monday night in March 1998, when, despite several new inches of snow and biting wind, five vendors showed up to work on story ideas. Early on, I found reporters from mainstream newspapers to work one-on-one with writers, and I held workshops on topics such as interviewing and reporting. Later, running the group alone, I introduced a workshop format: At each meeting we circulated copies of participants' writing to discuss, write together, and read our writing aloud. Over the next few years, the day, time, and focus of the group changed based on the writers' desires and interests. What became tradition throughout was the weekly meeting itself, the desire to find a public audience, and having lunch together. Eating before the meeting began was an important way to form community—and to be sure that no one was writing on an empty stomach.

The writers were a diverse group in terms of age, race, gender, sexual preference, religion, and life experiences. To describe the writers as "homeless" is to invoke certain stereotypes that were not always accurate. While the organization's mission was to serve people "who are homeless or at risk of becoming homeless," there were no specific rules about who could sell the newspaper. Anyone who decided that he or she was "at risk of becoming homeless" could become a vendor. This meant that many financially vulnerable people, housed and unhoused, chose to sell the paper. And as word about the writing group spread, a few people signed up to sell the newspaper in order to join the writing group. Homelessness was not, however, a meaningless concept in the group; many of the writers lacked stable housing. Some camped in parks, stayed in shelters, slept on trains, or rented substandard facilities.[5] Most struggled with additional material difficulties that constrained their possibilities for making a better life; defaulted student loans kept at least three writers from fulfilling their dreams of completing college degrees. Debt troubles and inaccessibility to legal representation kept others working in informal economies (like the street paper), which promised no job advancement, health coverage, or retirement benefits. Records of felony convictions rendered at least one articulate and hard-working writer unemployable, despite job programs for ex-offenders. A series of petty arrests and jail time caused other writers to miss out on job opportunities. Disabling conditions, such as blindness, mental illness, or substance addiction caused added difficulties for several writers, especially since adequate services were typically not available. Poor health conditions—ranging from HIV to hepatitis to easily treatable conditions like near-sightedness—coupled with lack of access to health care, dental treatment, or eye exams, diminished the quality of life for virtually every writer in the group. For one aspiring writer, an untreated kidney ailment resulted in death—one week before his appointment at a free clinic and months shy of his 49th birthday.

Writing in this group therefore amounted to an important but insufficient response to these sobering realities. Our weekly workshops did not offer any credentials or college credit. Letters of appeal did not unburden writers from student-loan debt. Articulate letters and recommendations did not allay prospective employers' fears about a felony past. Letters to health agencies freed up some eye exams and glasses, but there was never enough medical care when it was needed. The writers and I often discovered that our acts of writing were unable to bring about or transact anything definite. In addition, writers had to negotiate their desire to attend the writing-group meetings with often more pressing demands of earning money and negotiating the Byzantine network of state and social service institutions.

Public writing in our group began (or gained energy) at the point where transactional writing failed. When individual efforts at finding employment, housing, or another form of justice proved unsuccessful, writers turned to public writing out of frustration or a desire for social change. Early on in the writing group, these efforts took the form of individual articles testifying about events that writers either experienced or witnessed, such as "The Red Line is a Tough Place to Sleep, " an article that conveys a sense of homelessness as a difficult cycle to escape. Felix wrote this piece after leaving our meeting on a rainy night; he was unable to sell enough newspapers to rent a room, and had to spend the night sleeping on a Chicago Transit Authority (CTA) el train.

The Red Line Is a Tough Place to Sleep

Felix Meek

It's fun spending the night on the train going to Disney World, but I want to talk about what it's like to spend a night on a CTA train for a homeless person . . . .

I normally sleep on the red-line train. That means staying alert while sleeping . . . . Around 4 A.M . . . conductors leave the doors open a long time at each stop, letting all the cold air rush in.

While sleeping, many people are unaware they are being stalked by train robbers. These thieves sit back and wait on you to fall asleep. They surround the sleeping rider, front, back and on the side. First they touch him (or her) and ask him questions, hoping they are sound asleep. That's when they use razor blades to cut a sleeper's coat or pants pocket and steal their money or just reach over them and steal their purse or bag that might contain anything of value. Then they get off at the next stop. And when the rider wakes up, his personal belongings are gone and the other passengers just look as though they haven't seen anything . . . .

What a way to sleep . . . .

After a night on the train, my body feels tired but . . . I start my life as a homeless StreetWise salesman all over again. That's when bad health can come in—in six years I've caught pneumonia twice, colds, headaches, body aches and depression, which sometimes makes me doubt my reasons for living.

So, where does preparing for a job or going to a job interview fit in? Who . . . would hire someone who . . . spent the night on the red line? (Epstein and Mathieu 2000, 12)

Through this article, Felix sought to inform the public about a situation he could not ameliorate despite his best efforts. The writer had no direct goal, just a desire to testify about his life, in hopes that readers might see him and other people on the streets a bit differently.

Another member of the writing group, Robert, planned a book entitled *The World as I See It* that he hoped would help the public see *themselves* differently. As someone who often felt invisible on the streets, he felt he had a unique view of human behavior. Robert never finished the book but published several articles on the topic, including this one.

A Day of Selling *StreetWise*

Robert Dillard

Sunday: I was out selling papers on Diversey and Clark. The time was about 5:00 when this gentleman walked up to me and asked, "What are you selling?" I said, "Streetwise." Then he said, "I can't stand that paper, or you. Why don't you go somewhere else? The world would be better if people like you weren't out here everyday."

He was a white guy, about as tall as me (about six feet), wearing a T-shirt, gym shoes (it was kinda cold but he had on a T-shirt). Talked like he had a real nice education—he wasn't no bum.

I didn't respond. I kept saying to myself, I'm not going to let this guy make me mad. I just let him keep doing his thing. Then he said, "It's a stupid paper, it takes a stupid person to stand out in any kind of weather trying to sell a stupid paper like this. Don't you have anything better to do?"

I responded, "Yes, instead of me standing out here selling my paper, I could be at home writing my book. And by the way, if you don't mind, sir, I'd like to put you in my book. The name of my book is *The World as I See It*. May I have your name please."

He said, "No way."

I said, "I'll just call you Mr. John Doe. But I will put you in the book, because of the way you talk to me. And you kind of opened my eyes about what I want to say about the world as I see it."

He said he didn't care and he walked off. I told him, "Have a good day and God go with you." (Epstein and Mathieu 2000, 17)

This article and many others were circulated in several public forums—in the newspaper, through other local arts publications, and in public readings. "Vendor Voices" was a two-page section inside the paper set aside for vendors' writing. Once the writing group became established in the organization, we gained some editorial control of those pages. Discussions about publication choices became central in the group.

Pleasures and Perils of Streetwise Publishing

The public aspect of the writing group gave many members a small but important outlet to voice anger, discontent, joys, and triumphs. Publishing was a *de facto* privilege for the group and the reason most of the writers came to meetings, yet members spent much time discussing the advantages of publishing along with its limits and burdens. While most writers hoped for a wide audience, they expressed hesitations about going public. Some fears related to being read; others concerned not being read.

One writer feared that once his writing entered a public realm, he would lose control over the text and how it might be read and misread by audiences. Some writers worried that publishing controversial views might make them vulnerable to public attacks in whatever form. One member explained that writing was integral and necessary to his life, but that being read by a wide public was unexpected and made him nervous. Stella Fitzpatrick (1995), a facilitator of adult basic-education publishing groups in England, writes that feelings of attraction and apprehension are inherent to publishing, especially when the writers are in vulnerable economic or social situations. Writing and publishing, she asserts, is a constant negotiation between safety and risk, and she characterizes the experience as simultaneously "liberating and alarming," "a mixture of apprehension and pleasure" (11).

Writers frequently raised questions about the group's public identity and rhetorical persuasiveness. For writers who struggled between social invisibility and being seen in stereotypical ways, claiming a public space in print meant claiming a right to respond to issues and discourses affecting their lives, yet this public access came only as part of a homeless writing group. For many in the group, to claim an identity as a *published, homeless* writer was a conflicted one, to say the least. This issue emerged keenly when the writers began to find outlets for their writing beyond the newspaper[6] and received attention in local media. While planning a public reading and press conference for the publication of the group's writing in the *Journal of Ordinary Thought*, one writer said that he did not want to appear on camera because the news station to be present was carried by cable outlets in his family's hometown. He said, "I don't want them to know I sell this paper." The issue of affiliation also arose as we planned to release an anthology of the group's writing. Several members said they did not want the name of the newspaper to appear on the book's cover or if it did they requested the print to be small. They worried that potential readers might be turned off by the "homeless angle" and would not want to buy it.

Sometimes the risks of publishing extended beyond issues of identity to concerns about personal safety. One founding member of the group was in Chicago after fleeing an abusive husband in another state years earlier, so she had to make decisions about whether to publish using her real name or a pseudonym and whether to include photos, weighing the desire to be recognized for her work with her concerns that a copy of the publication might reveal her location. We used group time to discuss these difficult issues, especially near times of publication, public performances, and media interest. Some members chose to publish under pseudonyms, while others requested their photos not be taken. Others, however, strongly argued for the right to have their names and pictures used. This was a right, as they saw it, to claim a public identity as a writer—not a passive person, not a "bum," but someone possessing creativity and intellect.

Despite legitimate fears about being read in a public forum, writers additionally worried about not being heard at all. Was anyone changed or persuaded by what they read? We knew that roughly 25,000 people purchased the paper each week. According to street-paper readership surveys, readers listed writing by vendors as one of their favorite features of the paper. Yet, it was unclear exactly *how* readers were responding to this work or what conclusions they were drawing. Members wanted to get feedback directly, which is difficult when writing in print, especially a small newspaper.

The paper occasionally received letters to the editor in response to articles the writers' group had written. When writers sold papers on the streets they would get feedback from regular customers about their articles, mostly unqualified praise and requests for signed copies of the paper. While such responses were valuable motivations for the writers, they came sporadically and offered little information about the effects of the writing on readers. It was unclear whether the writing influenced how the readers perceived local issues and homeless people, or if they merely enjoyed and supported the fact that someone they saw as marginalized had chosen to write at all. One fear was that readers had overdetermined charitable responses to writing in the paper, in that it was read but appreciated in a paternalistic vein. The rhetorical challenge of the writing group—and of all street newspapers—was to offer writing that subverted tired stereotypes of homeless people without becoming a voyeuristic spectacle of individual struggles, pains, or triumphs.

One way we negotiated this rhetorical challenge of representing individual homeless experiences was to develop projects in which the writing group would collaborate. The first occasion of this group activity resulted from the trial of Gregory Becker, an off-duty Chicago police officer who shot to death Joseph Gould, an unarmed *StreetWise* vendor.[7] The group devoted seven weeks of the Vendor Voices pages to Becker's re-sentencing trial, writing in various genres and involving the reading public in an appeal to the judge, to which more than a hundred people and groups responded and publicly added their names. In the end, Becker received a shorter prison sentence than we had hoped but one more severe than we had feared. While it was impossible to know if and in what ways the outcome was affected by the letters sent to the judge and the public campaign, the writers felt it was important to speak out publicly together.

A desire for an audience and collaboration led members of the writing group to become interested in publicly performing their writing. This started with a few college and high-school class visits to the newspaper offices, for which the writing group planned readings. Later, through our group's affiliation with Chicago's Neighborhood Writing Alliance, the members had occasions to read their work in public forums like public libraries, the Chicago Cultural Center, and the Guild Poetry Complex. The performance aspect of the writing appealed to those writers who felt that the effects of print articles were too unclear or ambiguous. The desire for public interaction and dialogue helped spur interest in a full-length performance piece. Not Your Mama's Bus Tour was our most ambitious and outrageous public project. It was a theatrical bus tour of Chicago, narrated by members of the writing group, who told stories about their lives and their experiences in the city, in the spaces where they occurred.[8]

Not Your Mama's Bus Tour

Creating a theatrical tour of Chicago guided by homeless writers, for which we expected the public to pay $25, was a strange and silly idea in many ways. The possibilities for failure were many. The group had never attempted a project for which specific writers *had* to be present. At our public readings, interested writers just turned up, and we always had sufficient numbers. In this tour, we would have a specific cast with ongoing performance demands. No one was sure if we could—or would want to—accomplish them. Despite the risks, this seemed like an important public project for several reasons: (1) It was a concrete way to link the writers' stories with Chicago's city space in a format that would allow a powerful face-to-face interaction with a live audience. Unlike writing an article for a newspaper that people might or might not read, imagining an audience for the play was clearer for writers, because this audience would be physically present. (2) The bus tour could provide the writers with a public platform for raising political and social issues that affected their lives yet were beyond their individual control. Around that time, the group was especially concerned about citywide gentrification and Chicago's push toward a tourist economy, and how these priorities led to service cuts and decreased housing availability for low-income areas of the city. The bus tour was designed to co-opt (and parody) the city's tourist aims and provide a serious, yet humorous, counter-discourse to it. (3) Since we imagined a paying public for the tour, we planned to pay the writers/actors for their rehearsal and performance time. In this way, the writers would not have as many material constraints when choosing to work on this project. (4) This project would require the writers to hone a wide range of skills—writing for a public audience, proficiency with computers (to write and edit scripts), the ability to commit to a project and arrive on time, public speaking and performance skills, and the ability to collaborate on an ambitious project.

The tour came together quickly. With the help of a Dutch theater director and Chicago's Neighborhood Writing Alliance, our group planned to put a storytelling bus on the road within six weeks, to prove to ourselves that we could do it and to see if the public liked the idea. During the first three weeks, the writers scripted possible scenes, working from prompts I prepared. In the next three weeks we worked with a giant map of the city to determine which scenes were artistically and geographically possible, mapped a course, rehearsed scenes, raised money, found a bus, publicized the project, talked with reporters, and sold tickets. Our cast of a dozen homeless or formerly homeless writers-turned-actors kept to a rigorous rehearsal schedule. The writers negotiated a group agreement with the organization for payment for their writing and rehearsal and performance time.

The process was hectic and energizing. None of us was really sure that we could actually pull the project together. There were so many potentially crippling problems—actors not showing up, poor weather, lack of public performance permits, not to mention the possibility that the public would not respond well, or at all, to the event. We jokingly posted on the wall our ten biggest fears, naming and laughing at them as a way to take away their power. Days were spent editing and rehearsing scenes, while nights were spent driving through the city, planning the route, and timing distances from place to place.

On a warm and clear night in August 2000, a yellow school bus filled with press, friends, and supporters paused momentarily before driving northbound on Michigan Avenue toward Grant Park, the scene of the 1968 Democratic Convention riots, and the location of the first scene of Not Your Mama's Bus Tour. Curly, one of the two tour guides, announced the following to the 44 passengers on the bus:

> Ladies and gentleman, I'd like to welcome you aboard tonight and go over a few rules. According to the National Transportation Safety Board, we are required to tell you that:

This is not a Gray Line, Blue Line, or Happy Face Tour.

At 7:07 we will not strain our necks at Navy Pier to look at some McFerris Wheel and pay $14.95 for a sandwich named after a city 767 miles away.

At 7:18 we will not entomb ourselves in a stomach-turning elevator climbing to the 104th floor of the Sears Catalogue.

At 7:29, we will not pass Go or City Hall, where Richard sits only because his father sat all over this city.

At 7:38 we will not even discuss corporatized cows or public ping-pong.

At 7:57, we will not contemplate John Hancock in any form. The name alone indicates just how obscene it is.

And finally at no time during this tour will we stop at any McDonalds, let alone some Rock 'n Roll McDonalds, for a way-too-boring double-cheeseburger combo super-sized, as if there isn't already enough wiener envy in this city.

This is Not Your Mama's Bus Tour, but depending on your mama, this may be her kind of ride. Welcome aboard.

This introduction set the tone of the performance as both play and critique. Through humor and word play, Curly's introduction made it clear that this tour would show a different kind of Chicago to audience members, yet it would not be one lacking humor or pleasure.

Over the next two hours, the bus made six stops around Chicago: Grant Park, scene of the 1968 Democratic Convention riots; Maxwell Street, the birthplace of Chicago blues and a historic immigrant gateway and marketplace, now all but demolished due to the expansion of the University of Illinois at Chicago; a Gold Coast apartment building, where one writer had once been taken in by friends; the street corner where Gregory Becker shot Joseph Gould; Orchestra Hall, where one of the writers had performed at age 17 in an Irish dance troupe; and Malcolm X College. While the bus drove from place to place, the passengers heard stories told by two tour guides, as well as poetry, songs, and music. At each location, the passengers got off the bus and watched a scene based on a story from a writer's life.

Anaya, who was struggling with student-loan debt, performed her scene in front of Malcolm X College, one of several Chicago city colleges. Because she was nervous about the public exposure this event might bring, she was reluctant to disclose too much information about herself. We worked together to create a scene in which she could share certain information with the audience without feeling too exposed. We struck upon the form of a game, creating cards listing several topics about her life—some were areas she was willing to discuss and others were not. As the crowd exited the bus just at sunset, Anaya stood in a paved open courtyard, as a huge sign reading "Malcolm X College" was lit high above her head in the background. She smiled a radiant smile, sporting long braids and a bright purple jacket. Once everyone was gathered closely around her, she spoke:

> Hello everyone and welcome. You can call me Anaya. Anaya only. I am homeless. There are many stories I could tell you about my life and some things I don't want to talk about. So let's play a little game. To do so, I need two assistants. (She then chose two audience members.) On these cards are subjects related to my life—Family, God, Age, Childhood, Malcolm X College, Sex, Exercise, Drugs, Relationships, Recovery House, and Mental Health. If you choose a topic I am willing to talk about, this is the sound you'll hear. (To the first volunteer, she says) Please give us a sound! (Person makes a sound.) Thank you, let's give her a big hand. And if you've chosen a topic I am NOT willing to talk about, this is the sound you'll hear. (To the second volunteer she says) Please give us a different sound. (Other person makes a sound.) And two more rules: no pictures and no questions. Let's play.

When someone selected the card "Malcolm X College," the audience heard the following:

> I am standing just twenty steps from the door of Malcolm X College. But it might as well be 20 miles. Six thousand dollars in student-loan debt separates me from Malcolm X or any other college. How long would it take you to pay off this debt? For some people it might be two years, a year, two months, two weeks, or even one day. For me, it's been five years, and I still haven't made a dent. I have worked homeless and gone to school homeless. How can a girl who loves education and longs to go to college make her way when the earth trembles and the ground beneath her begins to shake?

Anaya's scene was interspersed with both polemical and utopian fragments, including singing, poetry, and monologue sharing personal information like the fact that she had never used drugs, was mentally healthy, wanted to wait until marriage for sex, and was a devout Christian.

At the end of the scene, she explained the game to the audience by saying, "I used to say yes to any request, providing any information, regardless of whether I wanted to or not. But now, I can say no. I am not my experiences, I am not my debt, and I am not my past. You can call me Anaya."

In this scene, Anaya was able to speak about the role debt was playing in her life, to educate the audience, without feeling a sense of shame or apologizing. For those few minutes, she literally controlled the game, and she reveled in the moments when audience members chose cards, such as "Age" or "Family," and she held up her laminated sign, "I don't want to talk about it." And in the moments she did share, she gained a sense of confidence that evolved over the length of the performances. Her previous reluctance to speak gave way to memorable performances, where she played with the audience while allowing them to assemble a partial tapestry of her life. Her game subtly played with the public's voyeuristic interest in the poor. The audience *had* to ask questions, and Anaya was in the role of saying yes or no, controlling the audience's desire for information.

This was just one example of the element of parody in the performance. The writers and I had agreed that the audience should not find the tour lacking in humor or artistic pleasure. Many scenes had nothing to do with homelessness at all, because the writers wanted the audience to see that being homeless was just one aspect of their lives; it didn't explain who they were or encompass their identities. Thus music, both recorded and live, dancing, poetry, and humor were all elements of the tour.

Later in the tour, the bus wound its way through Chicago's medical district, described by Curly as "the largest concentration of hospitals in the city, which ironically sits just east of the neighborhood in the city where the fewest residents have health insurance." He dryly added, "Well, at least they have a nice view of the hospitals." He went on to describe the procedure for seeing a dentist at the county hospital (for those lacking health insurance), which he described as "the only place in the world where people run to, and not away from, the dentist." The "Toothless Olympics," as Curly called it, was a process that begins with a qualifying phone call at 7 A.M. one day. The next day everyone lucky enough to get through on the phone waits outside a locked door, and when it opens they race down a series of hospital hallways to try to beat out the "69 other tooth-achin' qualifiers" to arrive at a desk, get a number, and wait several hours on "a hard-ass bench" to see a dentist—to have the tooth pulled. "That's right," the guide told the audience in an authoritative and reassuring tone. "The only dental care available at County is getting a bad tooth pulled. No fixings, no fillings, just pulled. So, remember everyone, don't forget to brush!" At that point, the masochistic song "Dentist" from *Little Shop of Horrors* boomed through the bus, while a cast member cheerfully passed out toothbrushes to passengers.

Through moments like these, the writers shared a view of the city and its bureaucratic procedures for dealing with poor people that most audience members had never seen, yet did so in a playful rather than heavy-handed way. And since the audience and actors were physically present together—in an un-air-conditioned school bus in August—this allowed for dialogue between writers and audience. One of the tour guides, for example, always asked whether anyone in the audience

had ever been inside Cook County Hospital. During the dress
rehearsal, when the casts' family and friends were aboard, many affir-
mative hands went in the air. Once the paid performances began, no
hand ever went up. The tour gave audience members a glimpse into
life at the county hospital. And by handing everyone a toothbrush, the
guide suggested that they too might find themselves on a "hard-ass
bench" someday, waiting for a free tooth pulling.

For its final scene, the bus stopped in front of Chicago's Orchestra
Hall, where Maggie would be selling newspapers, awaiting our arrival.
She refused to ride with the other actors in a car just in front of the
bus, assuring us that she would be waiting at the scene when we
arrived. Every night the tour guides and I would sweat out the
moments before the bus pulled up to the spot, fearing she might not be
there. Gee, Curly's co-guide, would even tell audiences, "Maybe we'll
see Maggie; sometimes she's out here selling newspapers," just in case
she wasn't there. Then there would be a pause as Gee looked for her, a
pause that seemed to me to last forever, though in reality it was never
more than a moment or two. "There she is," he ended up saying every
night. The audience filed out and gathered around Maggie, as she
stood on a busy sidewalk downtown on Michigan Avenue. My laptop
and portable speakers were quickly rushed out to provide musical
accompaniment. Radiant at sixty, with colorful headscarves and several shirts and skirts, Maggie commanded attention. With a portable
microphone, the guide introduced her and asked her why this location
was special. Every night her explanation differed somewhat, but it
always included her memory of dancing onstage at Orchestra Hall as
part of an Irish Dance troupe when she was 17. She usually said, "We
did a four-handed reel that night, but since I am alone here tonight, I'll
dance a jig for you all." At that, my computer started an mp3 file of
"Irish Washer Woman," and Maggie danced a jig with the lightness and
brio of a teenager. Through her words and dance, Maggie transformed
from a self-described "bag lady" to a joyful presence that captivated the
crowd each night. People far beyond our paying audience stood
around to watch and listen, so she regularly danced for hundreds. My
hope was that her performance—as well as the rest of the tour—
communicated to the audience that much history, talent, and beauty
reside in the people that one might see homeless on the streets.

Our group staged six two-hour tours over the course of three
weeks. Local media covered the event, including local TV news coverage, print stories in seven newspapers including the *Chicago Tribune*
(Chicago's largest daily paper), top coverage on a local theater website,
performances recorded by two documentary filmmakers, and reports
by two radio stations, including a 20-minute interview and news piece
on the local NPR affiliate. The reviews were all positive. One reporter

called the project a mixture of "Chicago history, street theater and candor" (Rumpf 2000). Another described it as bringing "an unconventional history lesson to life through street theater. At times, it is also a poetry slam, a jam session, and a sing along" (Vogell 2000). The headline from the theater website said, "This bus'll school ya. . ." (Buccola 2000). All the shows sold out, and the public responded warmly to the tour and to the actors. Audiences lingered after the performances, asking questions of the cast, and getting autographs. People called and emailed words of gratitude and praise. Of the twelve cast members, none missed a performance and almost no one missed a rehearsal, an unprecedented reality in the two-and-a-half-year history of our group.

Tactical discourse was the realm of the StreetWise Writers Group. Unable to equal or overturn the powerful strategic systems scripting their lives, the group created projects in various polemic and utopian forms—calculated pot shots, poetry, humor, critique and parody—as tactical responses to the systems framing their lives. Not Your Mama's Bus Tour parodied the present strategic power of the city and offered glimpses of possible other realities. During the weeks of rehearsals and performances, all the group members were committed to—and pushed each other toward—the impossibly funny and strange idea of a traveling theatrical bus tour narrated by singing, dancing, and speaking homeless people. The project temporarily rewrote the strategic mandates affecting the writers' lives. Twenty people of different ages, races, and economic groups worked together toward one vision of a yellow school bus. The writers negotiated their own work conditions. They were paid a living wage to share their wisdom and perform life stories, taking people to the actual city spaces where they occurred. More than 150 members of the paying public heard stories about living with debt, police brutality, discovering sexuality, and finding hope. Twelve homeless writers/actors received pleasure, good experiences, and a job for six weeks. They honed their writing skills in creative and engaging ways to directly and immediately address a public audience. And indirectly, the writers responded to the powerful records and institutions framing their lives. At its best, perhaps this fleeting experience allowed the writers and producers a glimpse of a different life, where work is a meaningful act of creation. Perhaps it gave everyone involved a bit of hope, to keep struggling and keep risking.

The tour attempted to upset conventional expectations about Chicago, bus tours, and homeless people. Unable to directly change the city spaces denied to the poor, the cast literally co-opted the city for two hours a night and turned it into an impromptu performance space.

Lacking the stable nexus from which to continue the bus tour in the long term, the project's power was tactical—short-term, with a beginning and ending point. There was friction within the nonprofit about how quickly the project came together and the writers' right to negotiate their own work terms. The organization's director threatened repeatedly to cancel the show and, in the end, only reluctantly let it go forward. During the first scene of our last performance, police arrived and threatened to tow the bus away for not having secured permits to allow people to gather. An attorney advised us that if the tour were to continue, we could be sued for playing music without paying royalty fees. The tactical possibilities of this wonderful project eventually began giving way to the strategic realities of laws, permits, and organizational dissent.

The end of this project also marked the end of my three-plus years at that organization. Our writing group continued in a similar form after I left, and a revised version of the tour has continued for several summers. After the performances, however, even the most well-intentioned audience members returned to their comfortable homes, while Anaya still faced her debts; a tooth that could be filled today is still pulled at Cook County Hospital. As a tactical project, this tour created flurries of press and moments of energy. But as de Certeau suggests, the effects of tactics are not clear or permanent. They must operate within temporal restrictions. Structural realities do not readily disappear.

Yet, despite the fact that this project did not have a clear outcome, it was still a meaningful act of creation. One performer described the time of the play as one of the happiest moments of her life. Another said, "This is real. In a world that is increasingly unreal or virtual, that's important." Another said, "It's art, and that's why it's important." After nearly three years working with the StreetWise Writers Group, I began to understand the hopeful aspect inherent in tactical writing. The writing of the group, especially in this project, was never a means for something else—a better job, a grade, a more just world. While many of the writers wanted to change their lives, get a better job, or change the world, all were aware of the slim likelihood that our articles or projects could accomplish that. Certainly, the writing always had an eye on someplace else: on a better future. Underneath it all was hope, a hope that maybe enough writing, publishing, and bus tours might change the world. Hope stirred the projects and prompted discussions and writing, but the work was an end in itself. In this group, public writing was a meaningful act of community. Writing was never a transactional means to something else. The pleasures of the collaborations, shared meals, discussions, and quiet moments of writing were enough, for that week. But how the group's writing changed any readers or the writers is unknown and even unknowable.

Public Writing, Social Change, and the Long Vision

Paul Loeb's *Soul of a Citizen* examines, in hopeful and practical ways, how social change operates and the role individuals play in changing the world. He claims—and shows through many examples—that social change is a mysterious process and that one rarely knows when he or she has affected another or when social movements really grow. Loeb argues that social change occurs through the actions and storytelling of many ordinary people but that the full impact of such work is rarely measurable, especially not in the short term. We change lives through our ordinary actions, through our writing, maybe; but change is a mysterious process, and to try to be effective publicly is a risk that requires hope. We may never know the outcome or effect of our writing, but, without overestimating our power, we have to hope that it does something. This is the heart of a tactical approach to writing: One works for and hopes for change in the powerful systems that script our society, but one does not look to transactional rewards as a needed extrinsic exchange for the act of writing. The doing of the thing itself has to be enough pleasure or reward, because being heard in a fractured public and making change in the world is a slow and unpredictable process.

According to Loeb, the ability to remain engaged in the messy, unpredictable process of public participation without burning out or becoming cynical requires a long-term vision that he refers to as "radical patience" (313–16). It also requires gaining meaning from the human interaction and community found in public action and letting go of the need for certainty:

> Fighting for our deepest convictions requires relinquishing control and accepting messy uncertainties. It demands working as well as we can at efforts that feel morally right, and then having faith that our labors will bear fruit, perhaps in our time, perhaps down the line for somebody else. "If you expect to see the final results of your work," wrote the journalist I. F. Stone, "you simply have not asked a big enough question." (Loeb 1999, 114)

Radical patience does not suggest that writing and public activism create no changes in the world but rather that they aren't easy to predict or measure. Loeb describes the experience of Dr. Benjamin Spock, who attributes his interest in nuclear disarmament to a group of mothers and children he saw huddled in the rain one afternoon years earlier on the steps of the Capitol. Those women probably never learned that their actions on that day—which likely seemed fruitless at the time—profoundly affected one person, who then became involved in influencing many others. Further, large-scale social change does not occur in equal or predictable increments. As Joanna Macy writes, "The moment before water turns to ice, it looks just the same as before. Then a few crystals form, and suddenly the whole system undergoes cataclysmic change" (Loeb, 106). Writers working in the public realm often need a long-term vision to get a sense of the impact of their work.

Assessing the Real Changes at *Real Change News*

An example of tactical street writing that has sought to assess its long-term public impact can be found in *Real Change News*, the Seattle street newspaper that celebrated its tenth anniversary in 2003. Its founder and director, Tim Harris, decided that this milestone was a good time to gather opinions of vendors, staff, and readers of the paper, in order to assess the first decade of the publication and plan for the second. *Real Change* wanted to know what readers thought of the newspaper and what, if any, effects it had had. The paper spent about $1,100 (and some free newspapers, to enlist the help of vendors) to pass out 3,000 mail-in cards to people buying the paper. Tim described the process: "There was a place on the card for vendors to write their ID#, and we would credit them two papers for every response card we received. We were hoping for 1,000 replies out of the 3,000 and got almost exactly that" (Harris).

What surprised Tim the most, when the results came in, was the number of people who were reading the paper and viewing it as as a critical source of information in Seattle. "We heard repeatedly through our interviews that we are respected and read by policy makers, and more than 40% of our readers say they read half or more of the paper." He owes the paper's credibility to the quality and consistency of the content: "I think we're credible because we're a newspaper and we more or less cleave to the journalistic form of separating fact from opinion, appearing to be balanced, etc. This would not be the case if we dismissed objectivity as a tool of the ruling class, or if we were the sort of paper that published homeless writing just because someone is homeless. Quality is key to being read and respected."

While Tim credits the paper's content, he learned from the survey that words alone aren't enough to make social change; they need to be placed within a context of human interaction and movement building:

> I think that without the vendors we'd be just another left-leaning paper of marginal impact on anybody, even the choir. People are led to the paper by the prospect of experiencing a momentary connection based on human kindness and compassion. Most people don't come

for the journalism, and seem a little surprised when they find that it's good. This, however, gives us access to a much broader readership than we'd otherwise enjoy, and those relationships are the foundation for any impact we have in the community. People say we have made a huge difference in the way people see poverty and homelessness here by humanizing the poor and keeping the issues in front of people. I'd like to believe that's true, and have some reason for doing so. (Harris 2003)

What *Real Change* discovered in its readership survey and through its first ten years of publishing is that its writing makes a public impact, even if it is sometimes difficult to gauge. Key to this effectiveness is a commitment to bringing important stories to the public attention and to writing in a balanced way that has allowed the paper to gain the public's trust over time. But in striving for effective writing and social change, the greatest effects are forged not on the page, but in making connections with people. Writing alone is insufficient to change the world, but in a context of human organizing and community building, writing helps bring about and give voice to many changes. Tim describes it this way:

I don't think journalism alone creates much social change, but I think a street paper is a good platform from which to extend other advocacy and organizing efforts. There are articles we've run that people still talk about, but none that I can name that directly created social change on their own. I think much of our impact has been cumulative. It's a question of hanging in, and being consistent with a quality paper that people can respect.

Classroom Public Writing as Tactics of Hope

The writing projects described in this chapter represent just a handful of experiences of a few activists and financially marginalized people; the purposes, audiences, and means of circulation of these writers would likely differ from that of writers working in large nonprofit institutions or with greater access to economic and social power. Their tactical writing serves specific rhetorical aims in specific times and places. Based on these examples, I would like to explore, in the remainder of this chapter, possibilities for classroom public writing as tactical acts of hope.

The Outcomes of Public Writing Are Mysterious and Unknowable

Viewing public writing by those without claims to mainstream power as tactical acknowledges writing as powerful in mysterious, uncontrollable, and playful ways. Rather than understanding writing as a clear transacting process, a tactical view marvels in the potentiality of writing while acknowledging the limits of its power. To view public writing otherwise asks students either to practice simulated documents that never enter the public realm at all (such as a letter to the editor that isn't sent), or to send out writing into the world without much rhetorical calculation about where or how it might make a splash. Without an appreciation of the unpredictable nature of public writing, dutiful students might be disappointed by their forays into the public sphere. A tactical view of public writing incorporates the unpredictability of the outcome as part of the process.

To incorporate an understanding of the tactical nature of public writing into a class, one could take time to introduce students to an understanding of how social change occurs and the role writing plays in that process. Paul Loeb's *Soul of a Citizen* is an excellent source to use with students to interrogate and understand processes of social change. Historical case studies can also be useful. For example, reading about the suffrage movement in the United States creates an awareness of the need for patience and persistence in assessing the transforming power of words and public appeals. Many of the landmark appeals for women's suffrage date back to the Seneca Falls Conference in 1848, yet the 19th Amendment, which granted women the right to vote, was not passed until 1920. Two now-canonized suffragists, Elizabeth Cady Stanton and Susan B. Anthony, died nearly two decades before American women earned the right to vote, but their speeches and written texts were key to that movement. This example, and countless others through history—including the anti-apartheid movement in South Africa, nuclear disarmament, and the anti-Vietnam-War movement—show that the rhetorical power of words within a movement toward social change often requires a historical view to assess. As part of asking students to engage in public writing, it is useful to help begin with a historical understanding of how public discourse has and continues to change the world. (See Eberly 1999 for more examples.)

Tactical Writing Focuses on Projects, Not Problems

Tactical writing employs a project rather than a problem orientation. A problem orientation operates from a negative space, in that it seeks to solve a problem, ameliorate a deficit, or fix an injustice. There is a transactional quality to it—if the problem is not solved or the injustice ended, the work will be deemed unsuccessful. A problem orientation runs the risk of leaving participants overwhelmed, cynical, and feeling weak. A project orientation, however, privileges creation and design. Projects respond to problems but determine their own length, scope, and parameters, instead of being defined by external parameters. C.'s group, for example, didn't seek to solve the problem of economic injustice; rather they conceived of their work as serial acts of design in the form of campaigns, rallies, or videos to make utilities more affordable. The *StreetWise* writers didn't take on homelessness directly, but through projects like the bus tour indirectly made things happen that *might* change the reality and perceptions of homeless people in their city.

The writing class can be imagined as an ideal time and space for public-writing *projects*, as a creative space in which interesting projects happen during the course of the semester. Geoffrey Sirc, in *English Composition as a Happening*, critiques composition's epistemic turn for causing the field to lose sight of the avant-garde elements of composing, thereby losing a vision of the writing classroom that allows "the inhabitants a sense of the sublime, making it a space no one wants to leave, a *happening* space" (1). While Sirc might view my interest in public writing as far removed from the avant-garde compositions of artists like Marcel Duchamp and Jackson Pollock on which Sirc's work focuses, I believe we share a desire to create writing classes that become exciting pedagogical writing spaces in themselves, without needing to appeal to an extrinsic result, exchange, or skill.

What kind of tactical public-writing projects can work in the classroom? Any examples I offer will not be determinative, in that each local space, class, and teacher will need to discover what kinds of projects would be engaging or relevant. Much of the most exciting work in composition today, however, shares a desire to reframe the classroom as a writing-project space. Michael Blitz and C. Mark Hurlbert's *Letters for the Living*, for example, descibes writing courses where students write books alone or in semester-long writing partnerships with students at another campus. Nancy Mack (2002) asks her working-class writing students to create multigenre research projects detailing some aspect of their background or home community. Derek Owens in *Composition and Sustainability* works with his students to explore and document stories and histories about local places—hometowns, haunts, and hangouts—as a way to participate in a public discussion about the health and sustainability of places. What these projects share is a focus on creating meaningful and innovative texts that work beyond themselves within the communities of the classroom and within the families and neighbors of the writers as well. Other writing projects that come to mind include oral history projects (Cassel 2000), public or campus events, or campaigns. Projects can also evolve through collaboration with activist groups, community organizations, or local nonprofits (Goldblatt and Parks 2000). Later, I discuss some writing projects in my own writing course (Chapter 3) and in a service project I helped create with college students, children living in a homeless shelter, and the Boston-area street paper (Chapter 4).

Tactical Writing Invites Collaboration and a Long Vision

Semesters are short, but the lives of public campaigns are long. How can the two work together? A tactical view of writing makes collaboration, both in the classroom and with local groups, an important way to turn writing classrooms into project spaces that can tap into larger movements. As any public writer or activist knows, any event, rally, performance, public debate, or newspaper issue comes about through the cooperation of many people and an ongoing agenda. And through those moments of cooperating on a project larger than oneself, one can find a great deal of pleasure and meaningful exchange. By co-creating with other people, one can find, in Loeb's words, "a sense of connection and purpose nearly impossible to find in purely private life" (1999, 5).

Students themselves are often great sources of information about key local and national issues. Student groups have recently been at the forefront of anti-sweatshop movements and other projects for global justice. In a writing course, if you choose an issue-related project in which all will have to participate, you run the risk of turning off students who either don't agree with or are not interested in the issue. If, however, you simply ask individual students to "go out" and "find a public issue" that they "care about," the risk is that they will never participate in either the pleasures or frustrating mystery of public writing in any communal or collaborative way. What I try to do in my classes is to create one or two projects that relate to ongoing issues familiar to me, and to allow students to participate in those or to choose something of their creation (see Chapter 3). I don't think any one approach is best; rather, it's important to know the pitfalls of any collaboration and make an informed decision accordingly. For students anxious to see the effect of their public writing, the requisite long vision for tactical projects might prove disappointing. If the collaboration reaches beyond the bounds of a classroom, one needs to assess realistically what kind of support or help a semester's worth of college students can provide to your campus or to a local community group. In this aspect, general guidelines are not useful, since the local needs and demands are key.

Writing instructors can play a key role in helping semester-long projects tap into ongoing campaigns. New class projects can extend or build on projects from past semesters. If an instructor has ongoing relationships with local writers or activist groups, new projects can develop as needs change. I say more about the role of the teacher/writer/scholar in the streets in the concluding chapter.

Tactical Writing Embraces the Imaginative to the Mundane to the Silly

I have learned from writers like C. that engaging in public work means doing many things at once—one day writing ritualized appeals for funding to state institutions or foundations and the next writing an article, poem, or press release. Forms vary widely, as do the rhetorical needs of the writing tasks. When asking students to write publicly in a classroom, we can draw on a wide range of rhetorical forms, from the imaginative to the ritualized. Writing a press release, an appeal to a judge, a grant proposal, a recommendation letter, a poem to be read at a public picnic, a newspaper article, an editorial—each of those acts of public creation places different rhetorical demands on a writer and creates different effects in the world. A tactical approach to public writing allows the rhetorical demands to dictate form, formality, and content. For example, in a research writing course I once taught on the topic of globalization, students first wrote academic research papers and then collaborated to revise their individual work into a class website about their concerns for the future. Each writer had to decide, in consultation with his or her peers, how to revise individual research into forms that would make sense and connect with an unknown audience on the Web. One writer, for example, transformed her research on the environmental impact of computer manufacturing into a quiz for visitors to the site. Another student turned his exploration into the effects of NAFTA on unionized workers like himself into a funny poem entitled "Afta NAFTA, what's next?" (In these and other tactical writing projects, questions of form also include visual design, especially if websites, books, fliers, or other public documents are created.)

As forms range, so does the level of seriousness and play. At times, as the *Real Change News* example shows, dedication, research, and journalistic balance can win the day. In tactical writing, however, humor often prevails by having a "subversive effect on the dominant structure of ideas" (Douglas 1991, 295). Even *Real Change* works to use games and humor in certain key ways to get their messages across. Their website (http://www.realchangenews.org) includes an interactive game, entitled "Hobson's Choice: The Game You Just Can't Win." Players enter a simulated world of homelessness and are faced with a fixed number of choices at each turn, and each decision leads to consequences that can improve or worsen the player's plight. For example, when faced with having no place to stay, a player might select "Sleep in your car" as an option, which leads to the following consequence: "Too bad, you're in Oregon where it's illegal to sleep in your car. Now you're in jail." If the player selects the choice "Call your lawyer," the response might be, "Too bad, poor people can't afford lawyers. You're still in jail."

The less reliable access writers have to institutional power, the more likely their exercises of tactical power will employ jokes and humor as "attacks on social control" (Douglas 1991, 295). In a classroom, teachers, students, and situations will dictate if and in what ways humor, games, or play are relevant, but tactical writing projects should be open to such possibilities.

Tactical Writing Has Clear Exigency, if Not Always a Clear Goal

As a project orientation suggests, writing projects succeed if they manage to create something that has energy. Tactical writing rarely transacts or accomplishes anything concretely.[9] The class, the project, the thing itself, should always have clear hopes and purposes while letting go of specific goals.

C.'s campaigns for affordable utilities, the various projects of the *StreetWise* writing group, and the past ten years of *Real Change News* are just three examples of the many ongoing public writing projects operating in the streets of our cities and towns. These writers draw from a range of rhetorical stances and appeals—anger to parody to balanced journalism—in order to use writing to intervene in public ways. They organize their work around various projects: a rally, the week's issue of the paper, a public reading, an open house, a public discussion of an issue, a trial, a bus tour. Each individual writing project is temporary but not isolated, in that it is a part of a movement or a campaign larger than itself. Each project garners energy and then ends, but during the process it is alive and engaged with the world. These public writing projects are tactical, and rely on hope and goodwill to go forward. They don't claim systemic change in and of themselves.

Seeing writing as a transacting tool (to credentialize or influence) frames writers as subjects who need to gain power in order or achieve something else. Seeing writing as a tactical act of hope acknowledges that power is something that all people, even the socially marginalized, already have. Tactical power is real, but it is unreliable, constrained, and its effects are often unclear. Claiming that power through acts of public writing is insufficient. It is an act of hope.

Notes

1. Some material from this chapter was taken from two articles. For more discussion of the StreetWise Writers Group, see Mathieu 2003 and Mathieu et al. 2004.

2. Writing teachers and theorists have responded to a desire for relevant pedagogy in many ways, including seeking to replace required composition courses with specialized electives (Crowley), creating expressivist pedagogies that ground inquiries in student-derived topics and ideas (see especially Elbow; Newkirk; Tobin), and prioritizing writing for peace (O'Reilly) and burning issues (Blitz and Hurlbert). See also Yagelski and Leonard.

3. See Isaacs and Jackson for a helpful overview of public writing in classrooms.

4. Also cited in Wells.

5. Researchers debates definitions of "homelessness" and offer varying estimates of the numbers of homeless people. See Jahiel; O'Flaherty (9–19); Jencks; and National Coalition for the Homeless.

6. Chicago's Neighborhood Writing Alliance, publisher of the *Journal of Ordinary Thought (JOT)*, was the group's primary outlet to additional public venues. May 2000 saw the release of an issue of *JOT* authored by the StreetWise Writing Group. See Epstein and Mathieu.

7. See Mathieu et al. 2004 for a fuller discussion of the Gregory Becker case and for questions about the identity of the writing group.

8. See Mathieu 2003 for more about this writing project.

9. There is not a clear dichotomy of transactional and nontransactional writing; rather the transactional ability of writing exists on a continuum. A law or other secure strategic edict operates with nearly direct performative power, in that its issuance creates material realty and names certain individuals as deviants. At the other extreme, a poem written by a homeless person, scribbled on the sidewalk, accomplishes nothing definite; if it affects a passerby at all, those effects are tactical. Much writing, however, falls somewhere in between. A grant proposal makes appeals to strategic power and might result in the transactional benefit of funding; but then again, it might not. A rhetorical appeal claims tactical power when its competent and timely completion does not guarantee any specific result. In a traditional writing class, competent and timely completion of work does guarantee a passing grade, which is why I characterize it as at least somewhat transactional.

Three

Street Life in the Classroom

*We need to move from grandiosity, PR, and guilt assuagement
toward making personal connections and linking personal stories
with issues in the political economy.*
      —Tom Boland, Founder, Homeless People's Network

*If I were teaching about homelessness, I would visit shelters, hang
out. I wouldn't necessarily stay overnight in a shelter because I
wouldn't want to take a bed away from someone really needing it.*
      —Marc Goldfinger, Poet, Writer,
                  Needle Exchange Counselor

The Pedagogical Draw of the Streets

Derek Owens (2001) asserts that a writing teacher has both a great privilege and responsibility when designing a composition course: "If the
writing teacher has the power to make students write and read about
practically anything, [he or she must answer the question] what then
are the most important things for them to write and read" (7). As I discussed in Chapter 1, many English teachers have turned to service
learning, public writing, and politically relevant issues as sources of content and sometimes audiences for writing courses. Probably the longest
standing and most contentious aspect of this public turn in composition
has been introducing social or political issues from the community, the

country, or the world as content into the English classroom. As a series of old debates make clear, scholars in the field of composition have heatedly disagreed about the pedagogical and political appropriateness.

In her 1992 article "Diversity, Ideology and Teaching Writing" Maxine Hairston writes about "a new model for freshman writing programs, a model that disturbs me greatly . . . [that] envisions required writing courses as vehicles for social reform" (180). She decries such an approach as a "regressive model . . . that threatens to silence students" and lists "names that you might look for" who are guilty of this social approach to pedagogy (180). A year later, several of those "outed" by Hairston as radical social reformers responded in print, including John Trimbur, who argued that the new model worrying Hairston wasn't new at all but represented "a move to reconceive (or perhaps restore is a better word) first-year composition as rhetorical education for citizenship and to place public discourse, as well as students' composing processes, squarely at the center of the curriculum" (248–9).

My goal here is not to rehearse this interesting, historical debate within the field about the role of politics in the writing classroom.[1] Rather, I would like to recast this debate not as a disagreement over politics but as a debate about the appropriate scope or space of a writing course. Hairston argues that the ideas and writing processes of students should delimit the appropriate reach of a writing class, while Trimbur (2000) argues that rhetoric, "that ancient trickster," has always defined the terrain of a classroom more broadly, to include public discourse and the wider world "by calling on students and teachers alike to look at how the language we use constitutes the world we live in, the differences that separate us, and what we praise and blame in our hopes for a better future" (179). Hairston's more expressivist, process-based approach argues for the classroom as the salient context for a writing class in which "the world" should enter only through students' own writing. Trimbur's social-rhetorical perspective broadens the scene of the writing classroom beyond the text, the writer, and the classroom to explicitly introduce the community and world in which writing takes place. A choice in pedagogy, then, inevitably leads to a teacher's definition of what Di Leo, Jacobs, and Lee (2002) call "the site of pedagogy," which they define as "the spaces in which interactions between teacher and student occur" (7).

More than a decade after these debates were published, writing teachers continue to answer differently the question of scope in a writing classroom. As a field today, composition seems organized around a wide array of answers, in the form of special interest groups, specialized journals, and composition scholars well known for defined subareas of interests, via a variety of technologies, pedagogical sites, and theoretical approaches to teaching. Amidst this heterogeneity of opinion about what constitutes the appropriate scope of a writing course, an increasing number of teachers introduce pedagogies that either directly or indirectly delimit the site of composition pedagogy to include civic or street life outside the classroom. Street life—a term I use loosely to refer to a wide range of social and political sites, such as cities and suburbs, homeless shelters, prisons, school systems, community centers, and gentrifying neighborhoods—finds its way into English curricula via introductory composition courses and themed literature and writing courses, as well as cultural-studies and American-studies offerings. The appeal for many teachers relates to urgency and relevance, as C. Mark Hurlbert and Samuel Totten write in *Social Issues in the English Classroom*:

> The English classroom should be more than a place where students
> compete individually and in isolation to finish assigned and easily
> consumable, easily categorized, easily gradable readings and writings.
> The English classroom . . . is a good place to begin reading and writ-
> ing and talking and listening together for a more democratic and eth-
> ical society and for a safer and healthier world. The English classroom
> is a good place for students and teachers to explore . . . the issues and
> conditions affecting this time and the public lives we lead in it. (2)

While defining the English classroom as a site of central civic and public importance opens up its possibilities, it also broadens the pedagogical site to include the lives and issues of those not affiliated with the courses themselves. The relevant context no longer involves only students and teacher, but also community members or other local constituencies. A classroom that invites students to connect their learning and acts of writing to concrete, local concerns can become a site for personally meaningful research. But the classroom also becomes a more complicated place, where the variables defining successful teaching and learning no longer only involve those taking part in the class. When the scope of a course becomes broader, so too do the number of issues and concerns a teacher must consider. That's both the good and bad news.

This chapter aims to outline some of the practical and ethical implications of bringing subject matter from the streets into a writing classroom and seeks ways for pedagogies to be more responsive to specific pedagogical sites. Questions in this chapter include: How much must a teacher know about an issue that he or she brings to a class for writing and discussion? Why and how should we invite interested people in the streets to take part in the planning or teaching of our courses? How does one decide how to frame a local issue and choose what material to include? What, if anything, do we owe to constituencies outside the classroom when we seek to represent their struggles in our classes? When we invite guests into our classes, how do we incorporate and compensate them ethically? In defining course questions around local issues, how does one draw the boundaries in order to consider the influence of broader, more global economic and political concerns? How do we help our students and ourselves gain useful social maps to help navigate the complex terrain of local and global issues? And finally, how should broadening the scope of a course to include street life change questions of assessment and course redesign?

Based on a *tactical* orientation of *hope* (see Chapter 1), such questions can only be answered in terms of local and changing circumstances and cannot claim general truths. As a way to explore these questions, then, I refer throughout this chapter to my two semesters' experiences teaching Literatures of Homelessness, a rhetoric and composition elective course. I describe my course as a heuristic case study, to allow a specific grounding for asking questions about defining and teaching a course that brings street life into the classroom. I do not offer my own teaching as a "model" approach to integrating street life in the classroom, but rather, I hope my experiences illustrate the promise and limitations of teaching about the issues and struggles of a group of which one is not a member.

Literatures of Homelessness

When I was hired out of graduate school into a university English department, my new employer asked me to design and teach an elective undergraduate course based on an "area of expertise" from my dissertation. This pedagogical flexibility was an extraordinary opportunity, and I was pleased to think through the challenge. I first suggested a course on community writing and publishing, in which students would review theories of literacy and then research, and perhaps participate in, community writing projects. This idea was considered a bit too specialized for undergraduates, and I was encouraged to think in terms of a literature course.[2]

The homeless writers I knew from *StreetWise*[3] wrote a great deal of what I considered to be literature, as did journalists at street papers around the world. In my years of work with street papers, I had read a lot about homelessness—novels, memoirs, policy studies, ethnographies. After my first course idea was refused, the words, "How about a class called Literatures of Homelessness?" spilled from my lips, without considering what such a course would entail. For whatever reason, the course was quickly approved, and before I had even begun to think through the ethical, political, and pedagogical details, 40 students had enrolled. Like it or not, I was going to be teaching students to read and write about "homeless literature," and I had to decide how to bring this street issue into the university classroom.

My first response was panic and self doubt. I had only the most tangential personal claim to a "homeless" identity: After a house fire when I was eight years old, my family spent a week bouncing among neighbors and hotels until my father found us an apartment for the nine months it took to rebuild our home. Thanks to my father's income, good home insurance, and welcoming neighbors, I never spent an uncertain night anywhere. Who was I to be teaching a course like this, and how could I do it ethically?

Despite never having been homeless as it's commonly understood today, I did have some experiences that others had not. I had been working with street papers and homeless writers for five years at that point, both as a journalist and writing teacher, thinking and reading a great deal about homelessness. But I had not yet directly linked this work with my writing classes at the university. Was I "qualified" to be teaching students about homeless writing? And what would I want them to learn anyhow? I wasn't exactly sure, and I only had a few months to figure it out.

Jumping into a politically loaded course without fully thinking through its ethical, practical, or pedagogical implications is not uncommon for teachers of writing and other socially oriented courses. Good intentions often precede good thinking, especially given the realities of scheduling, hiring, and course planning. And that's all right, as long as thinking doesn't end at good intentions, which, as we all should know, pave the road to hell. It is imperative to get beyond the initial blush of satisfaction in doing communally or socially engaged work and ask the difficult questions that follow.

Seeking Advice from Community Experts

The summer before I first taught Literatures of Homelessness, I traveled to San Francisco for the annual conference of the North American Street Newspaper Association (NASNA). There I visited with other street paper writers and editors, as I had done for the past five years, had conversations, held workshops, and dreamed up ideas for making our ragtag network of local newspapers function on a national and international level as a journalistic voice covering issues of poverty and homelessness. That year, I also had other questions of my own: I needed to ask my colleagues their thoughts on how to teach issues of writing and homelessness in a university classroom.

During those four chilly July days (San Francisco is seldom warm in the summer, as Mark Twain reminds us), I drank more coffee than I needed and inhaled lots of secondhand smoke talking with street-paper workers, those who had been homeless and those who hadn't, to get their feedback on what, how, and why to teach about homelessness in a literature course.[4] To bring homeless writing or any other form of street life into the classroom, it's useful and even liberating for a teacher to begin from a point of admitting limited knowledge. Learning when, how, and whom to ask for advice is a key skill for expanding the scope of teaching into areas of street life.

Two people with whom I began conversations in San Francisco became invaluable in my course planning: Tom Boland and Marc Goldfinger. Both were longtime residents of the Boston area, where I was about to move and teach; both had experienced homelessness in their own lives and were working in different advocacy positions. If you were to pass Tom on the street, you'd be reminded of Willie Nelson, only a less country, more Haight-Ashbury version. Slight, somewhere in his fifties, with sleek long gray hair and a white beard, Tom laughingly admits that the teenagers who pass by while he's having a smoke outside his hangout, the 1369 Coffee Shop in Cambridge, often call him Willie. I first met Tom at the previous year's NASNA conference, where we co-presented a workshop on homeless activism and the Internet. He discussed the Homeless People's Network (HPN), an online discussion group that he founded and moderates, which is open only to people who have been homeless.[5] We had spent several hours the day before the workshop riding on a bus through Edmonton, Alberta, discussing access to computers for homeless people and planning the goals of our workshop. During the workshop itself, Tom's gentle articulateness, well-informed political views, and sincere belief in the value of consensus made him an excellent teacher and facilitator. I knew during that workshop that I had found a mentor from whom I would have much to learn.

I can't remember when I first met Marc Goldfinger, but it must have been at a street-paper conference. He was working for Boston's *Spare Change News* as a poet and sometimes editor; his writing often tackles in frank and evocative ways his more-than-a-decade's struggle with heroin addiction. Marc looks a bit like Jerry Garcia, with a salt and pepper beard and warm smile. He sports a trademark uniform consisting of fedora, jeans, suspenders adorned with political and nonsensical buttons, and one in an impressive array of T-shirts, many homemade, sporting artsy images or leftist political messages. Marc's humility and warmth shines through especially at his poetry readings or when talking about his spouse of two years, Mary Esther. Through hard work at recovery, supported by his writing and lots of spiritual work, Marc has become a substance-use counselor in a needle exchange program in Cambridge. When I first visited him in his office, he pointed to the printed results of his criminal background check, which are taped to the wall of his work cubicle. "All those arrests, that's the diploma that matters most to the people I work with. I don't speak out of a position of higher authority; I was right in their shoes" (2003).

Through many conversations with Tom and Marc, as well as other poets, writers, and editors at the conference, I started exploring the range of questions, readings, and projects that could frame my class. I didn't want to take too much time away from the work at hand, so during breaks I would offer to buy a cup of coffee and ask general questions, like, "What are the most interesting or challenging books or articles related to homelessness that you have read?" I also did some research on possible student projects by discussing ongoing initiatives in the network (like plans for a poetry anthology and a news service) to explore if there might be useful ways to connect my students to this work.

When I met with Marc I asked him what he thought someone should know in order to teach a class about homeless writing. He recommended a humble orientation, one of co-inquiry with the class, coupled with as much research beforehand as possible:

> If I were teaching about homelessness, I would visit shelters, hang out. I wouldn't necessarily stay overnight in a shelter—because I wouldn't want to take a bed away from someone really needing it— but then again having that experience might offer something. It's a tough question. If you're teaching a course, you don't want to offer misinformation. Share what your credentials are and aren't. This is who I am; this is what I know. Present the class as a two-way deal: I can give you some information, but you need to check it out, see if it's accurate. (Goldfinger 2003)

The conversations that began in San Francisco continued once I arrived in Boston. I met with Tom to discuss a proposal: that he work with me a bit over the summer and during the semester, advising me and offering feedback on the course. I told him that I had a decent understanding of the politics and community existing around homelessness in Chicago but that I knew nothing of Boston, other than my acquaintance with him and the folks at *Spare Change News* and an unspecified commitment that I would start working with them. I admitted that I did not yet know what, if any, financial resources I might have access to, but that I would do my best to compensate him equitably for his time and expertise. He said that his expenses were small and that he would be happy to participate in my course. I also invited Marc to come to my class when his schedule would allow.

Grounding a course in political or social matters of street life demands more than just pedagogical preparation. It demands an understanding and grounding in the local place, local issues, and the current moment. As "rootless professors" (see Owens 2001, 72–74) who often travel great distances for jobs—either because of geographical relocation or long commutes—many instructors like myself lack the ability to gain local knowledge of a pedagogical site (including knowledge of the students I would be teaching and the communities from which they came) before beginning to teach there. One pedagogical response might have been to wait to teach a course grounded in local issues and spend time working in and getting to know my community. Since that wasn't an option for me—and such ideal visions are seldom options for teachers—I came to rely on advice from friends and local community advocates like Tom and Marc to help orient me to the place and discover issues about which I would be teaching.

A key question in approaching those outside the university for their help with our work within the university is *how*? Are there right and wrong ways of asking for input and help? While there may be few clear right ways, there are plenty of wrong ways, according to many advocates I have asked. Too often faculty show up on their doorstep *after* they have an agenda, *after* defining a project, a class, or a research idea. When academics enter a scene already carrying an agenda, they may fail to acknowledge and genuinely interact with people as individuals and instead view them only as means to an end. According to Tom, the best way for academics to connect with those in the streets is to begin without an agenda, to arrive and experience the work and struggles on a personal and human level. Requests for help, he said, are most effective if they grow from personal relationships. Referring to our working relationship, he said, "Our first contact had nothing to do with your course. I got to know you as a young woman on a bus. As a person. As someone with whom I would be working on a common project [the homeless technology presentation]" (Boland 2004). As is often the case, it is easier to call upon people you know for help than it is to ask a stranger. The better we know, and are known, in the streets and communities where and about which we want to teach, the easier it will be to make connections and frame issues well.[6]

Framing an Issue

Asking questions and getting advice is important, but the teacher is the teacher and at some point must make decisions and plan the course. A teacher ultimately has to ask and answer the following questions: What is this course all about? What questions do I want my students to ask and think about? How one rhetorically frames the questions defining a course that includes local issues—especially politically charged issues like homelessness—plays a key role in delimiting what can and can't happen in the course.

Questions of what I hoped to accomplish in my course were further complicated by the student demographic I would be teaching—predominantly affluent, majority white, majority traditional-college-age undergraduates. That's not to say that there might not have been students with direct experience with homelessness in the classroom, but it did mean that homelessness would likely only be an abstraction to most if not all students, and that anyone with direct experience would potentially want to keep quiet about it.

During my planning, I tried to avoid what I saw as two dangers. First, I feared that the course could easily become a voyeuristic exercise in exoticizing an absent and abstract other, where we would read about homeless people's lives as a way to learn titillating details and assure ourselves that "we," the safe classroom audience, would never end up that way. A second fear was that the course could become a boring exercise in liberal political correctness, where students would feel that the only acceptable responses would be empathetic, and through their work they would generate one-dimensional, mechanical responses of pity or superficial gestures of charity.

Tom Boland helped me clarify these concerns by relating his past experiences with being asked to speak in academic situations. He said that depending on how the questions guiding a course, conference or symposium are framed, certain kinds of responses are ruled inappropriate while others become expected. Sadly, it wasn't difficult for Tom to recall an example of a less-than-positive experience:

> Once, I got invited to [a local university] to address the question, "Should we give money to panhandlers?" I had no say in how this question was framed; the discussion was rigged from the start. I tried to explain in my remarks that, historically, any group that the powerful has wanted to keep out has been described as abusing material goods. How they framed this question played right into that: Aren't all homeless people lazy or greedy? These stereotypes are constant—the homeless are always cast as endangering specters . . . . Too often, if you're asked to speak in a class, you get put in an Oprah role. You're expected to confess, to be in a fishbowl where everyone can examine your inner stuff—the poster child or cripple that everyone is looking at and thinking, "Thank god that isn't me." The object of pity. There is a sense of polite disgust. (Boland 2004)

Tom's remarks show the limitations of being invited into a classroom and asked to weigh in on a simply constructed pro/con debate—whether or not someone should give spare coins to panhandlers. He said that framing the question in such a way put him in a no-win position. To advocate giving money or withholding money from people on the street who represent themselves as needy raises the issue of greediness, and, more importantly, it prevents putting on the table more nuanced questions of housing costs, policy decisions, the value of charity, individual responsibility, etc.

In her remarks at the 2003 New York Conference on College Composition and Communication conference, which coincided with the United State's official declaration of war on Iraq, Diana George discussed the importance of bringing "hard topics . . . . (gun control, reproductive rights . . .)" back into the classroom—and I think homelessness would fit within this list—but in doing so to "refuse to submit to the familiar terms of the question" (2003, 346). Instead of allowing social issues to be confined to the tired debates of pro or con, George suggested asking tougher questions like why (Why are debates about death penalty largely constructed around whether or not someone is guilty?) and how (How can one survive while living on the minimum wage?). She argued, "I'd like my students to pay attention to how the media decides what is newsworthy and what goes unquestioned . . . . Where is the public discussion? Where is the public debate? I want my students asking those questions as a part of understanding how language works, how argument is made or not made, and why it is crucial to question the language of power" (347).

George's remarks are vital in helping teachers think through our challenge, which is not about choosing a topic but choosing *how* to frame the inquiry into a topic. In the end, I chose to focus my class on questions related to popular depictions of homelessness in mainstream media and how they are reinforced or critiqued by academic writing and writing by people who have experienced homelessness. Rather than making the course an interrogation into the lives of people who become homeless, I framed the course as an exploration of the role of writing and literature in shaping popular views and material realities of this issue. I showed Tom a draft of the syllabus, and used his questions and feedback to fine-tune its language. The central questions of the course, articulated on the syllabus, centered on relationships among the issue of homelessness, the literature written about it, its writers and readers, and the world in which these works circulate:

> What is the relationship between literature and the society in which it is written: Does literature merely reflect society, or does it create, shape, or oppose it? Do popular books and news accounts about homelessness affect the world in any way? Do they help raise readers' consciousness and help to bring about an end to homelessness? Or do they naturalize homelessness as something that always will (and thus should) exist? How does a piece's genre or author affect its impact on readers? What are the different aims and effects of, say, a policy study or a piece of poetry? What differences (if any) exist in depictions

of homelessness rendered by mainstream journalists and novelists, academics and artists, and homeless writers themselves? These are some of the questions of this course. (Boland 2004)

Despite my preparation, I did not manage, ahead of time, to side-step all of the pitfalls in framing the questions of this course. While I *thought* that I had set up the course as a site for dialogue and discussion about the issue of homelessness and the power of writing to intervene in positive or negative ways, at least two students during the first semester articulated in evaluations that a politically correct atmosphere dominated the class. I tried to counter this the second time around by including a segment on popular films about homelessness and incorporating role playing, which required students to raise questions from the perspective of Hollywood producers, land developers, business owners with homeless people sleeping in front of their stores, etc. These changes helped encourage a more multivocal classroom, but certainly didn't banish that specter totally. Involving guest speakers helped a great deal, and also allowed the guests, and not me, to embody a position that challenged students' views.

Who Speaks? Who Pays?

In trying to set up a classroom that engaged questions about rhetoric and homelessness in complex ways, I knew I didn't want to be *the* voice that challenged mainstream conceptions of homelessness. I also felt obligated to invite into the classroom speakers for whom home-lessness wasn't an abstraction, and compensate them for their time.

In the course of four years at *StreetWise* newspaper in Chicago, I had heard repeatedly from homeless or formerly homeless vendors of the paper who had been invited to speak at a university or high school classroom. They would take most of a day, navigating public transportation, arriving early at the school, giving a talk, and answering often personal questions, only to be thanked in a heartfelt way and sent away empty handed. While it's true that these men and women agreed to speak to a school class without promises of money, it's also true that the teachers turned a blind eye to the material realities of the speakers they invited to their classroom. From talking with street-paper workers from around the U.S. and abroad, I have found that such an oversight is not only possible but commonplace. In fact, many street papers have done what we had to do at *StreetWise*: create a speaker's funds within our own organization, to help compensate vendors and employees invited to classes or community groups. While such internal funds are useful and recognize the value that public speaking about homelessness can bring to a community, the impulse to compensate classroom speakers should not be so one-sided.

Tom Boland's personal experience coincided with what I saw in Chicago:

> Probably less than half the times I've spoken at classes or conferences have I been compensated. And most of the time when I was, I hinted my way to it by talking about poor people not being compensated. In a sense, I've had to beg. [The reply to my request is often] "we don't have the money in the budget." You don't have $40 for a homeless speaker? It's not that you don't have it; it's that it's not a priority. (Boland 2004)

In universities, one's time tends to be compensated based on one's status. Prominent writers and scholars are paid large sums to give an hour's lecture, while graduate students and adjunct workers dare not calculate their per-hour rate for fear of never wanting to get out of bed again. Such a system isn't new, nor do I think that merely pointing it out will change it. My only hope is to highlight that, as teachers, we sometimes replicate such a system by assuming that community activists, nonprofit workers, and people occupying vulnerable economic positions will *want* to come and speak to *our* students, help *us* do *our* job, and do so without compensation. If we want people in the streets to help us take part in our teaching, how can we to make it worth their while? While I think reciprocity is a complex process (as Powell and Takayoshi suggest), one must have a mindfulness about the debts we incur when we invite community members into our classes. Return gestures might mean, for a nonprofit, a donation to the organization. It might mean helping to write a grant application. It might mean setting up a student exchange that meets a specific need. If a person is financially vulnerable or works for a community group that raises funds, it should mean at least offering reimbursement for travel costs.

When I discussed this issue with Tom and Marc, both corrected me by saying that the central issue isn't about money, it's about recognizing someone's efforts and honoring their presence. Tom explained it this way:

> In my first visit to your campus you put me into your whole day. We conferred beforehand. I addressed your class. Then we went to dinner, attended a talk. You brought me in fully. It takes a long time to travel on public transportation—three hours—more than an hour should be scheduled for that person. If you invite a member of the community to the class, treat them like an honored guest. Have them address some other group. Send them over to the scholarship office. Introduce them to your colleagues. Make it worth their while. If a

prof were to come to speak, they would meet the dean, have a meal. Don't hustle [your speakers] out the back door. In a sense, it's the social context in which the talk is set that matters. It's the honor in an honorarium that matters. And also recognize the material needs— reimburse at least for transportation and child care. At least help me break even. (Boland 2004)

Marc also expressed that reimbursing for transportation is an important gesture, one that makes it clear that the teacher or institution recognizes the needs in a person's life. Beyond transportation, he felt that there are many other important ways to compensate a visitor: "When people have a little bit of income, it's too easy to give money. Time is the most precious commodity any of us have to offer." (Goldfinger 2004)

This discussion about money is not to suggest that underpaid faculty should dip into their own pockets and pay large speaking fees in order to bring community members into their classroom. It does mean that this issue must be considered and discussed. And if universities benefit from connecting their classrooms to the street (through public relations, student satisfaction, whatever) they should at least be asked to pay for such a benefit. And even if speakers refuse any compensation, it is still thoughtful—and ethical—to offer.

When I first asked my department for help bringing homeless speakers and advocates to my classroom, I got lucky. My department arranged a $300 budget for me, from which I could compensate Tom and Marc and a few others for speaking to my class. I told the speakers the financial and student resources I would have access to, and they let me know what arrangements would work for them. We talked through topics on my syllabus and we arranged class topics and days to visit. As someone who had done graduate work at nearby Tufts University, Tom said he was happy to be in a classroom again. In the two semesters I taught the course, I managed to bring six individuals into the classroom to teach with me and arranged student interviews and phone calls with about a dozen other individuals. It was a relief to know that *I* did not have to represent or embody all knowledge about homelessness for my students, and that with creative use of resources, I could invite colleagues into my class in ways that worked for them.

What specifically did Tom, Marc and the other speakers bring to my class? As Tom spoke to students about his views on writing, the Internet, laws affecting homeless people, and shelters, the dynamic in the classroom changed. As he himself admits, he has a "formula and approach to talking about issues of homelessness developed over 15 years." His radical critique of, say, the shelter system or mainstream media reporting brought an informed and experienced point of view and embodied it in the classroom, which allowed me to frame the discussion rather than assuming responsibility for the content of alternate rhetorical positions. Marc's poetry, coupled with an arresting personal demeanor that celebrates the virtues of humility and personal reflection, won over the class and helped challenge some of the ideas we had read in the mainstream media about homeless people. A long and important discussion developed around his reading of "God Help Me":

God help me

to be a cool breeze on a hot day
a warm pocket in a biting wind
a handhold on the face of a sheer cliff
a bowl of rice in the hands of a hungry child

Help me God

to be the tremor in a gunman's hand so the bullet misses
to be a cup of water in the desert
to be the hole in the net so the dolphin escapes
to be a still mind on a stormy day

God help me

to be the size of myself, nothing
less and nothing more.
and when I look into your eyes
to see who I am dwelling in you

Help me God

to love, to know
that I am not better than you
and I am not worse than you
I am not as good as you
I am you.

for Thich Nhat Hanh (Goldfinger 2003, 33)

Drawing the Boundaries of the Local

In designing a course that focused on homelessness, which is a local and international issue with a range of political, economic, and social causes, I had to choose what to include within the borders of this issue. These decisions caused me to ask how does one define and demarcate the boundaries of a complex local issue? Where do local causes or effects blend with broader causes in places far away, which one might call global?

Much scholarship in cultural studies and composition today discusses and theorizes questions and pedagogies related to local concerns; at the same time, there is a preoccupation with globalization and things global.[7] In their collection *Articulating the Global and the Local*, cultural theorists Anne Cvetovich and Douglas Kellner (1997) assert that an important relationship exists between *local* and *global*: "Configurations of the global and the local constitute the economic, political, social, cultural and even personal narratives within which individuals increasingly live and die, define themselves, and experience the world today" (13). Despite the importance and centrality of the theoretical configurations of *local* and *global*, these terms often appear as vaguely defined binaries. In a U.S. context, *global* is often understood as what exists *out there*, as in outside the U.S., often in heavily indebted poor countries. For example, one higher education magazine devoted an issue to the theme "Toward a Global Vision," which consisted of articles toting the value of studying abroad. I fell into this trap of understanding the global as far away a few years ago when teaching a research-writing course on globalization. Students wrote on topics like the environmental devastation caused by computer manufacturing or the lives of workers in the *maquiladora* garment factories on the Mexico-U.S. border. While these projects were worthwhile, we had a hard time seeing or naming ways global forces were changing life in our city—except for the obvious advantages of cheap computers and ready-to-wear clothing. In other words, it is easy to overlook the global causes of local social problems and to define the effects of globalization as that which can found only by leaving the U.S.

Framing the global as something only existing far away risks making it exotic, abstract, and either irrelevant or unstoppable. It allows us to miss how globalization is rewriting our local spaces in both positive and deeply troubling ways. When teachers, or our students, examine local spaces, we can overlook a lot if we don't explore how the local is formed and sometimes overdetermined by broader economic and political forces. Cvetovich and Kellner (1997) assert, "Our challenge is to think through the global and the local by observing how global forces influence and even structure ever more local situations and ever more strikingly. One should also see how local forces mediate the global, inflecting global forces to diverse ends and conditions and producing unique configurations for thought and action in the contemporary world." (1–2)

The challenge, then, is to help ourselves and our students see the interaction and interdependency between local and global forces in creating the world we live in. And this challenge is complicated by the gap that exists—in theory, in terminology, in understanding—between the dichotomies of the local and the global. In *Spaces of Hope,* David Harvey explains that contemporary theoretical discussions of society have focused a great deal of attention at the polar ends of the local-global scale by offering two opposite discursive regimes: *globalization* and the *body,* which is "surely the most micro from the standpoint of understanding the workings of society" (15). The problem, according to Harvey, is that little theory connects these discourses of local and global; there is a gap when connecting individual bodies to larger movements of capital.

In teaching about social issues in our classroom, when we raise issues of local relevance, where and how do we connect these local situations to global trends, cultures, and economic movements? Can we connect a locally experienced social issue like homelessness to a broader global system without framing the system as utterly totalizing and unchangeable? Can we explore how trends in homelessness are caused by forces greater than individuals without erasing individuals or their lives?

When I started teaching Literatures of Homelessness, I knew I wanted to include a discussion of the way changing economic arrangements were rewriting my city and the options for homeless people. This meant that *I* had to become clearer about the connections between globalization and local incidents of homelessness. My students, when face to face on a street with a homeless person, wanted to know what went wrong; why was this person homeless? Students knew one kind of answer: stories—of mental illness, drug addiction, laziness, or individual bad luck. But they wanted to learn a more complex story, one that related individual decisions and local realities of homeless people to broader economic and cultural shifts—and I wanted to rhetorically frame such stories but not lose or overwhelm the class. My own education came in part through reading Saskia Sassen's scholarship on the idea of "global cities," hubs of transnational capital, like New York, London, and Tokyo, that literally must be rewritten spatially in order to accommodate skyrocketing demand for luxury office and residential complexes and to house the executives of the lucrative FIRE industries (Finance, Insurance, and Real Estate) what Sassen sees as the vanguard of globalization (2002). Sassen notes that global cities include "a consolidation of poverty and extreme physical decay" and that appropriating a "growing area of the city for high-priced . . . redevelopment has contributed to a sharp increase in homelessness" (260). I chose not to include Sassen's writing in my class because it is quite abstract, but her work helps me clarify ways to connect individual local homeless narratives to the larger cultural narrative of globalization that is being written today.

Mapping the Local and Global

In *Millennial Dreams*, Paul Smith writes, "America has no collective history, only personal anecdotes." He argues that one's understanding of civic life today is guided by "anecdotal image[s] and the private conversation" (200). Awash in these disconnected narratives and images, individuals often end up uncertain or overwhelmed when trying to understand and intervene in the world around us. Once we recognize the complexity of the world, it's easy for it to seem unnavigable. We lack a clear conceptual map to help us find our way. Fredric Jameson (1998) argues in his essay "Cognitive Mapping" that "the incapacity to map socially is as crippling to political experience as the analogous incapacity to map spatially is for the urban experience" (353).

When we open up the teaching of writing to issues of immediate concern to life on the street, the challenge becomes making the classroom a dynamic site for finding meaning in a culture that often appears fragmented and disconnected. One of the goals of my course was to help students map connections between "local" issues of homelessness and the cities, nations, and world in which we live. A desire to help myself and my students map these connections underscored my choice of readings and assignments. In that sense the "scope" or "scale" of a piece of literature became as important in my selection process as issues of genre, audience, and the persuasive appeals and ethos of the writer. In addition to asking students about how the form, context, and writers' ethos shape a piece of writing and its effects on readers, questions about scope became important too: What is the relationship between the scope or scale of a piece of writing and its rhetorical effects in the wider world? How do local, individual stories affect readers? How do broad, trend-oriented pieces seek to persuade or affect readers? How do we as students in the course connect local stories to broader, global studies?

While the readings varied each time I taught Literatures of Homelessness, I always selected a range of popular depictions of homelessness (through fiction, film, and news media), then shifted toward academic and non-mainstream works ranging from policy study, ethnography, documentary, and experimental art. Next came memoirs, poetry and street-paper articles, many of which offer first-person responses to the popular depictions.[8] Students were asked to read and write responses to each work in a dialogic journal—which would be circulated in class so that others could reply to their questions and responses—as well as write two papers.[9]

Questions of genre and rhetorical appeal led to some interesting class conversations. Students discussed, for example, whether it was useful to critique how popular books and films portray homelessness, debating whether people would pay to be entertained by a movie with homeless characters who weren't "wacky and wise"[10] or didn't have a heart of gold, like Joe Pesci in *With Honors*. We developed a role-playing panel in which each student portrayed one of the following: the producer of *With Honors*, an audience member who loved the movie, a homeless man who was denied a part as an extra in *Curly Sue* because he wasn't dirty enough,[11] and Ken Loach, a British filmmaker who believes that portrayals of homelessness are meaningless unless they offer solutions to the problem.[12] Rather than settling on one conclusion, discussions like these opened up issues of popular portrayals of homelessness as an important cultural and rhetorical situation.

Questions of rhetorical appeal ultimately coupled with questions of scope: Students discussed how a broad, economic study, like Joel Blau's *Visible Poor*, provides extensive information about general trends but presents its discussion of numbers without stories of individual people. On the other end of the scale, a memoir, like Lee Stringer's *Grand Central Winter*, engaged students through humor and detail but has its own limitations, as one student wrote: "It is what it is . . . . He is only one man, whose story I felt was compelling and beautifully written, but I am constantly conflicted with the notion that none of these stories offer any action. I already know how bad I feel and how that feeling doesn't even compare with life on the streets . . . . what do I do now?"

This important question—what do I do now?—was one I tried to answer both through class projects, which I discuss below, and through several readings that, in my mind, helped students map connections between local and global incidents of homelessness. One recommended article is Rene Jahiel's "Homeless Makers and Homeless Making Processes"; another is Roslyn Deutsche's "Kryzstof Wodiczko's *Homeless Projections* and the Site of Urban 'Revitalization.'" Both of these articles work somewhat differently with scope, seeking to map out broad terrains and connect cause and effect, local and global.

Jahiel's article examines homelessness from the top down, starting not with homeless people but with the pressures that help lead to homelessness, caused by housing markets, landlords, the job market, and the medical and social-service sectors. Jahiel writes:

> Homelessness does not occur in a social vacuum. In general, the events that make people homeless are initiated and controlled by other people whom our society allows to engage in the various enterprises that contribute to the homelessness of others. The primary purposes of these enterprises is not to make people homeless but, rather, to achieve socially condoned aims such as making a living . . . . Homelessness occurs as a side effect. Yet it is a consequence. (269)

Jahiel coins the term "homeless makers" and maps out people in the housing, employment, public assistance, and health-care sectors who engage in economic investments that have the unintended effect of adversely affecting the livelihood of vulnerable groups of people. "Economic investments," he writes, "also represent economic disinvestments" (293).

This article allowed students to connect some individual narratives with the economic policy studies we read. It mapped out various pressures and causes of homelessness—including pressures exerted by universities and other large nonprofit institutions to buy up available land and reduce housing stocks. Students found the range and approach of the information to be useful but a bit overwhelming. We talked about the process of mapping the visual to make sense of the verbal, which led to some of the final projects.

Deutsche's article relates the public debate around plans to revitalize a single local space, Union Square, a small park in New York City, to broader economic changes and public responses. Union Square had fallen into disrepair, and Deutsche displays the rhetorical strategies of architectural historians and city planners to justify redevelopment by blaming homeless people and then creating conditions that led to further homelessness. Deutsche explains that city planners invoked homeless people as the cause of urban decay in documents arguing for reform, by portraying the park as a once-glorious place now accented with a "derelict relieving himself" on its faded statues (3). In addition, city planning documents remained silent about the amount of low-cost housing this renovation would eliminate. In the public review process that led to the renovation of Union Square, the city was required to submit statements describing "the potential environmental effects" of this project (46). Planners created highly detailed and technical policy documents about noise level, air and water quality, and traffic circulation. Deutsche explains that no mention was made about the housing that would be destroyed or the number of people displaced from the area. In fact, part of the developers' requirements for the project was the demolition of a large single-residence-occupancy hotel in order to put up a luxury office tower. Deutsche contextualizes this one renovation within a changing city that between 1976 and 1984 lost more than 100,000 blue-collar jobs and destroyed the majority of its low-cost housing of last resort.

The renovation of Union Square Park was sold to the public as "crime prevention" (37). What this actually means, according to Deutsche, is that revitalization increases the number of homeless people, who can no longer live in cheap housing because it is torn down. At the same time, the rhetoric seeks to push those same people from the streets, in order to preserve renovated parks and monuments and to hide the poverty.

In addition to this useful case study, Deutsche adds to this debate a discussion of public art and its ability to resist the rhetoric of urban reform. She describes "Homeless Projections" by Krzysztof Wodiczko, an exhibit of photographs in a local gallery that focus on the monuments in Washington Park. Wodiczko seeks to reinsert homeless people (or *evicts* as he calls them) into the discussion of the park and the statues and does so by projecting light onto the statues at night that gives the illusion that, for example, a statue of a soldier becomes a homeless man begging with a cup.

Through this article, Deutsche frames public space as terrain shaped and contested by a range of interests and discourses. In class we used the article to understand the technical aspects of urban spatial reform and to consider the role of public art to affect or critique public policy. Wodiczko's work prompted the class to have serious and engaged discussions about the efficacy of public writing and art as part of their analysis of globalization. Many saw Wodiczko's response as an important, although insufficient, part of the story; as one student wrote:

> [Wodiczko's] effectiveness comes in introducing a new vision to a community that would otherwise ignore the implications of revitalization. Using monuments against themselves makes the message all the more powerful because everyday objects are turned into extraordinary objects, which illuminate a terrifying past . . . . [T]hough it seems extremely important in Wodiczko's project to draw attention to that which would otherwise be ignored by the general public, the problem is that he suggests no solutions.

These two articles helped begin the process of mapping a more complex local story of homelessness, one that connects causes with people, and policy to places. To do so, it's important to look at both the strategic rhetorical practices of cities and multinational interests, but also at the tactical responses by artists, homeless people, and students.

Projects as Tactical Writing

One fear in creating a socially oriented course that takes on issues from the streets is that students, now armed with cognitive maps that help them understand an issue with greater complexity, will feel *less* rather than *more* able to respond in positive ways. In my course, I didn't want to leave my students' question "What do I do now?" unanswered.

The desire to connect classroom learning with social action or engagement has been at the heart of the rise of service learning in many disciplines, including English composition. I take up the question of service learning in the following chapter, but for now it's enough to say that I had reservations about my ability to create a traditional service-learning component in this course with which I could feel comfortable. Instead I wanted students to apply the rhetorical skills, mapmaking abilities, and knowledge they had gained during the semester to create a final project that in some way sought to affect the world outside the classroom regarding homelessness. I offered a wide range of options and possibilities for the students and encouraged them to work individually or collaboratively. Each project had to be proposed in writing, discussed in a conference, and approved by me. Additionally, in conjunction with each project, students wrote a brief paper reflecting on and contextualizing the project, its place in the world, and why or how it matters.

As I argued in Chapter 2, tactical public writing often assumes a project orientation over a problem orientation. Tactical projects represent small, temporary, and insufficient interventions into some rhetorical sphere, usually acting with clear objectives as defined by the project, but often lacking measurable external gauges for success. Tactical projects tap into existing debates and campaigns and define small interventions into that debate. It was in this spirit that I asked students to use their imaginations to create *something* of substance. I offered many suggestions, possibilities, and connections; the students responded with creativity and innovation. To show how the idea of tactical projects, which I outline in Chapter 2, can be realized in the classroom, I describe the range of projects students developed in these courses, which can be categorized as mapmaking projects, artistic projects, journalism projects, pedagogical projects, and service projects.

Mapmaking Projects

The concept of developing visual conceptual maps relating to an abstract social issue appealed to several students. Map projects combine visual and textual information to help students and others understand local connections between homelessness and homeless makers. One student created an alternative map of Boston's Freedom Trail, which denoted sites of resources for homeless people and sites of local homeless-making projects, such as large land redevelopments and businesses opposing legislation to build low-income housing. The handsome, folded, color map parodied the original Freedom Trail map well, and the student said she planned to make copies and mix them in with existing Freedom Trail maps at tourist kiosks in Boston.

A student group took up Jahiel's claim that colleges and universities often play a key homeless-making role by buying up available land for expansion and failing to house students on campus. This issue is especially relevant in Boston, a university-saturated city where rental housing is costly and difficult to find. The group created a wall map entitled "Boston College as Homeless Maker." Incorporating an actual Boston road map, students added vast amounts of data about area rental rates as well as local university enrollments, endowments, and the percentage of students not housed on campus. Along one edge, the map chronicled snippets of the published responses by community members critical of Boston College's relationship to its Brighton neighborhood. Not merely a critique, however, this map displayed a series of practical solutions and recommendations to the college. It was presented to the entire class at the end of the term, and one member of the group discussed the proposal with the head of campus housing. The impressive laminated map now hangs in my office above my desk.

Other mapmaking projects included a neighborhood map documenting rental costs, with a legend comparing minimum monthly expenses in Boston and mimimum-wage earnings; a memorial map of an artists' collective in Providence, where the student had temporarily lived, which became vacant due to eviction and gentrification pressures in that city; and a mobile on which the writer connected the story of her own life—and her family's near-homelessness upon emigrating from Puerto Rico—and the homeless-making forces identified in the Jahiel reading. These students who created these "maps" combined visual and textual information to help themselves, their classmates, and sometimes those outside the class understand and orient themselves to the issue of homelessness. Their work supports Gunther Kress' claim that "Information which displays what the world is like is carried by the image; information which orients the reader in relation to that information is carried by language" (1999, 76).

Artistic Projects

Other students pushed the connections between visual and verbal information to develop artistic projects. A photography minor took a series of portraits of vendors, staff, and the physical spaces at *Spare Change News*, and at Haley House, Boston's Catholic Worker House, which also provided homeless services. She conducted interviews with vendors and staff, and assembled oral-history profiles of each person she photographed. In conjunction with a photography independent-study, she printed and displayed the photographs and text in a campus gallery and held a public opening. Several of her photos and profiles also ran in *Spare Change News*.

Another student wrote a short story based on his best friend's experience with drug addiction and near-homelessness. He printed and distributed the story to every member of our class and discussed his reasons for writing it. Two other students helped me compile and organize submissions for an anthology of poetry collected from street papers across North America. This was a project that I had started and the students' organizing skills and outsiders' eyes were useful in moving it along.

Journalism Projects

Since I am actively involved with Boston's biweekly street paper, *Spare Change News*, I knew the publication and its needs. As a result, I was able to meet with the editor and brainstorm possible stories that students could cover. More than a dozen students wrote and published articles in *Spare Change*, including news coverage of a statehouse rally, a profile of a free library literacy program, investigations of how homeless children attend school, book reviews of children's literature about homelessness, film reviews, interviews with staff and residents of an area shelter, and overviews of the number of homeless children in our state.

One student became interested in the writing of David Abel, a *Boston Globe* reporter who frequently covered homeless issues in unusual and potentially disturbing ways, such as profiling individuals on the street as content to be homeless.[13] The student was curious about Abel's views and understandings of homelessness. She asked me if she could develop a project that involved inviting him to our class and organizing a conversation with him. I said I wasn't sure that he would agree to visit but that she could ask. She did; he accepted. His talk in our class, and the students' discussion with him, was one of the most complex, disturbing, and engaging classes of the semester.

Pedagogical Projects

Several students planning to become elementary or high-school teachers were interested in devising teaching aids or curricula about homelessness. Three students wrote, illustrated, and assembled their own children's books about homelessness; the results were amazingly professional and engaging. Their reflections on the books showed how deeply they thought through a variety of issues, most centrally a desire to inform children in ways that made them see change and action as possible.

One student played *Real Change News'* online game, *Hobson's Choice* (see Chapter 2), and interviewed Tim Harris, the game's creator, for a paper exploring the role of games in educating children about social issues. She and a classmate created a board game, while another student created a classroom interactive game, both designed to introduce children to the challenges of homelessness. Several other students created lesson plans and teaching units around homeless issues.

Two students with leadership roles on campus organized discussions about homelessness on their dorm floor or in their volunteer groups, using readings and ideas from our course. One student organized a large meeting of student volunteers on campus and invited Tom Boland to speak. Another student created a handout and presentation to try to change her boyfriend's views on homeless people.

Service Projects

Several students did projects that got them off campus and working with those we met during the course. One student, adept in technology, agreed to work with Tom Boland once a week for two months, providing computer support to help Tom keep the Homeless People's Network (HPN) running. The student wrote a report on HPN and evaluated the value of his service; Tom evaluated the student's work and conferred the grade for the project. Another student agreed to volunteer as a copy editor at *Spare Change*, which meant agreeing to commit to a year's work, not just a semester, as requested by the organization.

The second time I taught the course, a year after moving to Boston, I created Kids' 2 Cents, a project in which I took a group of students to a local shelter to run a weekly writing and art group for the children housed there. The children's writing and artwork contributed to an annual special issue of *Spare Change*, entitled "Kids' 2 Cents." (See Chapter 4 for a fuller discussion of this project.)

I describe these projects as tactical in that they were small but not insignificant interventions designed to *do* something, whether that something was to inform, entertain, or question. They often combined textual and visual appeals and had a specific rhetorical audience in mind, whether it was the class, members of the campus community or people outside it. When the work benefited groups outside the campus, such as the Homeless People's Network, *Spare Change News*, or the North American Street Newspaper Association, the idea for the work initiated outside of campus. Like the work of the activists I profile in Chapter 2, these tactical class projects represented creative, fleeting, and insufficient responses from which few direct claims could be drawn. But leaving aside certainty, one enters the far more interesting realm of possibilities: We ended the class with a hopeful consideration of the future by imagining what these projects *might* have spurred, created, or helped make happen.

Evaluating a Course with a Critical View of Hope

> The false future is all that which repeats itself a hundred or
> thousand times in the future. It is indeed future but there is
> nothing really new in it. On the other hand, genuine
> future contains a Novum, which always has a tendency, a
> possibility, or a probability that opens up the horizon. We
> are safe with the false future, for it is like looking forward
> to going to sleep in a bed that we know is there. But the
> genuine future involves risk, because we are not certain
> what lies out there beyond us. We must imagine, grasp the
> tendency of the Novum and dare to move ahead with it.
> —Jack Zipes, writing on Ernst Bloch

A strategic (rather than tactical) approach to teaching imagines course design as a process that strives for a syllabus that works; course redesign then amounts to a desire to continue the course, changing it in some ways to incorporate a few new texts or assignments. Positive student course evaluations indicate a green light to continue in the future as one has done in the past, a license for repetition.

Desires for replication and even standardization are widespread in teaching, and often respond to pragmatic needs and overwhelming teaching loads. I would argue, however, that once one's teaching directly intersects with the lives of people who are not part of the teaching institution, a strategic desire for stable excellence must be replaced with a tactical desire for hopeful innovation. If one teaches a course that intersects with issues in the streets, life in the streets and those issues don't stand still. Neither do the lives of those who intersect with the course. And so evaluating a course tactically means placing innovation and movement at the center of the course, with a goal to creating something genuinely different each time. Newness isn't a goal in itself—it provides a means of ongoing inquiry, allowing the teaching to maintain a hopeful and humble orientation to the future and to the current world.

Change, however, need not be random. As teachers, we have useful, standard tools for assessing our work and planning revisions: midterm evaluations, end-of-semester evaluations, feedback from peers, class observations, etc. Literatures of Homelessness was quite different both times I taught it; course evaluations from the first semester helped me change and reframe the readings and seek a less one-dimensionally politicized atmosphere. Midterm evaluations during the second semester helped me rework student presentations to be more useful to the class. End-of-semester feedback helps me revise again in the future—perhaps in using the journal responses in a more specific or limited way and rethinking the readings or early writing assignments.

Too often, however, teachers of socially oriented courses stop here, with student evaluations and responses. While the needs and interests of students are important in a course, they are not the only relevant voices. The needs, feedback, and impressions of classroom speakers and people connected through class projects must also be considered. So must the changing street scene: What issues, debates, projects or campaigns are important now? How have the lives of the people with whom I am working changed? How will the class and its projects evolve in response to these changes? These are additional questions that a tactically oriented course must ask and answer.

Information I gained from colleagues and speakers helped change my course, as did current events. The second semester, Tom Boland's availability was more limited. Marc Goldfinger, conversely, had more time and became a more important figure in the class. A legislative campaign to create affordable housing was submitted for a voter referendum the first time I taught the course. The second time, a homeless woman, who happened to be a close acquaintance of one of the class members, was found dead in a clothing donation bin outside a shelter on a winter morning; she had fallen while climbing in, seeking warmth when area shelters were full. News accounts wrote nothing of her life, only of her death, as a "Homeless Woman Found Dead in Bin." That issue and several other news reports on homeless issues helped make the rhetoric of the mainstream media key that semester. The Kids' 2 Cents Project, which I discuss in the following chapter, began around the second time I taught the course; it responded to a direct need of *Spare Change,* and I felt more able a year after arriving in Boston to begin such a project. This writing group has continued a year and a half beyond its beginnings in the course and is currently not connected to any course. When I teach Literatures of Homelessness again, I will rely on current volunteers and shelter staff to help me decide if the project should remain independent or again fall under the umbrella of the course.

One can only make specific decisions about specific courses in the present moment, and all decisions are contingent with regard to resources, time, space, students, local issues, needs, and interests. When working from a temporal, tactical orientation, very few general rules can apply. Based on my experience and interviews with friends, however, I can offer these few tentative recommendations:

- Start in the personal connection. Get to know people, issues, and communities before seeking to connect a course or research project to them.

- Seek input in framing questions. It can be liberating and eye opening to admit one's limited knowledge. When you have personal connections with the streets about which you are teaching, getting input and advice is easy.

- Invite and honor all guests. Bringing community members from the streets into the class can have a positive impact on the course. All those we invite to our classes deserve to be honored, and it's up to the instructor to be sure that all guests find that their visit was worth their while.

- Consider the global economic implications/forces defining local issues. Helping ourselves and our students map and navigate the local effects of an issue as well as the global and local causes can help lead to a more nuanced understanding of the world.

- Consider what a project orientation instead of a problem orientation allows you and your students to accomplish. Projects should begin with community needs and not merely seek out places to serve.

- Seek feedback in addition to student responses and be willing to revise and reconsider course design. Students are an important, but not exclusive, constituent to consider when evaluating a course. We need to ask those *about* whom we are teaching—and hopefully, *with* whom are teaching—how we are doing and be willing to listen to their answers. We need to change and adapt our courses to changing spaces and times.

A tactical approach to bringing street life into the classroom is time consuming. It is not efficient. It is risky. It is not practical. It is not easily generalizable. Given the job structure of many teachers, it may not be sustainable. But to create a rhetorically and spatially responsive pedagogy is hopeful and engaged, and dares to seek something new. It constantly inquires into its own ethics and efficacy. As teachers, we need to decide if and how we want to define the scope of a writing class: Do we want to be bringing street life in the classroom? If so, are we willing to engage how inefficient and complex that can be?

Notes

1. For a nice synopsis of these arguments, see Anderson.

2. This situation represents a common challenge for composition and rhetoric faculty, whose areas of specialization can more easily be considered methodological rather than "content" areas in the traditional literary sense. When English departments are dominated by literature faculty,

composition and rhetoric faculty are challenged either to teach norma-
tive courses in composition or to articulate literary areas of "expertise"
that are recognizable both to colleagues and students. So while this
course is described as a literature course, I designed and taught it as a
rhetoric and composition course.

3. See Chapter 2.

4. I want to thank Anitra Freeman, Michael Stoops, Tim Harris, Linda
   Larson, Fran Czajkowski, Nigel Kershaw, Kari Lyderson, Marcia Rizzo,
   Mel Young, Norma Green, Marc Goldfinger, and Tom Boland for talking
   with me during that conference about the course.

5. See http://aspin.asu.edu/hpn and Chapter 5 for more on HPN.

6. Even knowing only a few people or one organization can help one get
   locally oriented. I learned that by knowing a few well-connected people
   and working with a locally recognized organization like *Spare Change
   News*, I could talk and work with individuals and organizations that
   might have otherwise responded distrustfully to a professor.

7. For questions of the local, see for example Baker, Jr; Goodburn; Owens;
   Berlin 1996; and Downing, Hurlbert, and Mathieu.

8. Popular depictions included novels, such as *Street Lawyer* (Grisham) and
   Ghost Country (Paretsky); a nonfiction essay, "Following Nancy Home"
   (Lawson); newspaper articles covering homeless issues from *The Boston
   Globe* and other newspapers (students did Lexis Nexis searches for their
   hometowns); and mainstream Hollywood films such as *With Honors, Fisher
   King,* and *The Caveman's Valentine*. Academic and policy-oriented texts
   included *Shelter Blues* (Desjarlais), a critical ethnography of a Boston shel-
   ter; analytical essays from *Reading the Homeless* (Min); *The Visible Poor*
   (Blau), an economic study of the scope and prevalence of homelessness;
   Shadow Women (Bard), case studies of hidden homeless women by an academic who was once homeless herself; and policy reports by organizations such as the National Coalition for the Homeless and the U.S.
   Conference of Mayors. Documentary films included *It Was a Wonderful Life*
   and short films by artist Krzysztof Wodiczko. Personal accounts included
   Grand Central Winter (Stringer) and *Travels with Lizbeth* (Eighner). For a full
   syllabus, visit my website at http://www.paulamathieu.org.

9. The first paper was a five-page analysis of a depiction of homelessness in
   a popular medium, such as journalism, film, or television, including
   what is present in the text versus what is missing, who speaks, what
   kind of data or information is presented, and how the issues or questions
   are framed. Rather than requiring judgments of texts, this assignment
   asked students to understand how the texts work and what kinds of
   arguments or realities they depict.

   The second paper, one semester, asked students to read and review an
   additional text about homelessness (from a list of more than 100 that I
   provided), and the other semester, asked students to research a question
   related to homelessness by relying not on popular sources but on policy

or academic sources. The goal was to use reading and writing to learn and share information with the class.

10. In *The Fisher King*, a television executive (John DeLancie, better known as Q from *Star Trek Next Generation*) who is developing a sitcom about homeless people called *Home Free* describes the characters as "wacky and wise."

11. See Ellis.

12. See Petly and McKechnie.

13. See Abel.

Four

Students in the Streets

True democratic campus/community partnerships—partnerships that strive to meet the needs of a community, as defined by the community, that are of high quality and sustained involvement, that involve students, faculty, and staff and community members—will be a key marker for higher education in the millennium.
—The Campus Compact Wingspread Conference

I've learned the hard way. Now when I get a phone call from a university professor or student, I don't reply.
—Fran Czajkowski, Executive Director, Homeless Empowerment Project

. . . . [T]he "right" form of service learning can only be decided upon by specific actors in particular contexts struggling with the possibilities and dangers involved in acting in communities beyond their classrooms.
—Aaron Schutz and Anne Ruggles Gere

Coming Clean About Service Learning

I want to come clean up front. I get nervous about initiatives to expand and institutionalize service-learning programs across universities and throughout the field of composition. I didn't always feel this way.

I first encountered service learning as a "community partner," while working at a "service site" in a nonprofit organization. At the time I was also a doctoral student in composition and rhetoric. I thought my double perspective of insider in both a university and a local nonprofit would help make service-learning connections successful for our agency and the students.

I was wrong.

The following stories of service-learning experiences that I encountered—and helped create—as a service recipient attest to the complexity of creating viable, mutually beneficial community-university partnerships. These partnerships require a great deal of familiarity, adaptability, and communication, all of which is often lacking in the world of semesters and top-down service-learning programs. And even with familiarity, adaptability, and communication, service projects frequently encounter difficulties and run aground.

One day a service-learning coordinator from a local university phoned up the nonprofit street paper where I worked and talked with me about possible connections. I was excited. Running a writing group and computer-learning center for homeless and formerly homeless street-paper vendors, I had several ideas for possible student projects—in our library, writing group, computer lab, or even working with the editorial staff to help create the weekly newspaper.

At first, signs were promising. I was invited to partner with an English course. I prepared handouts; I even used clip art to make them look appealing. This involved brainstorming possible activities and coordinating possibilities with editorial staff—two hours' work. Then I took a train to the university, another 40 minutes once I found the building. Then I sat through the class while projects were outlined. Turns out, I was sitting with workers from several other nonprofits, from which students would *choose* one site to serve. Suddenly and unbeknownst to me, my organization was part of a popularity contest, and we weren't doing well. In the end, homelessness didn't win. Didn't even come close. The children's group and the clothing exchange were big winners. One student came and talked with me as I sat alone with my handouts; I think she felt sorry for me. After our talk, she said she was "kind of interested." I left the class—now more than four hours of my day had been devoted to this—optimistically reassuring myself: "Hey, one good student. She'll be great. She can work in the Center and we can plan for future classes. Smaller is better. We'll all learn a lot."

The next day the student emailed me, saying she was dropping the class. I never heard from the teacher.

Several months later, I got a call from the same service-learning coordinator. I told her, "Look, I think this is important work. I think we can make some interesting connections. But my last experience wasn't so encouraging."

She listened and said little, lots of silence. Then she said another faculty member was seeking connections. Could I come up with possibilities?

I emailed another list of options. Two weeks, three weeks, a month went by. I was busy with other work. Then she called again. "The faculty member loves the idea of students working at your organization." Great, I thought, now a better fit. "But . . . we're not sure the activities you mentioned will be useful for our students."

Now I was quiet, not sure what to say. Finally, I said, "Well, I can be flexible. What did you have in mind?"

"We thought the students could follow around homeless people while they sell the paper."

"OK . . ." Another long pause. "And then what?" I asked.

"Then they could write papers about it," she said.

This was getting awkward. "OK . . . but I'm a bit unclear. How will that help us?"

Back to her as the quiet one. "I'll get back to you," she said. End of call. I never heard from her again.

So at this point, you could say, "There's nothing new here. We know all this. Your story represents poor planning in a 'Writing About' service-learning model.[1] Rookie mistakes. We've learned from examples like these and moved beyond this as a field. We're sorry for your inconveniences, but your story doesn't help us much. We now know better, and besides, you never actually had a service-learning course work with you, so what do you know anyhow?" I hear you.

I do know, however, that when a university like the one I dealt with has an institutional mandate to get its students "out there," serving, these kind of missed connections are more rather than less likely to occur. How many missed connections or inconveniences happen in a typical day or week as universities scramble to make new connections, many of which never get off the ground? How many bridges do universities routinely burn while claiming to serve their communities? The university I spoke with had a big service-learning program. They had funding, a full-time coordinator. But rather than creating successful partnerships, this structure created a situation in which someone who did not know local organizations *had to* create multiple community connections, making it possible—and perhaps necessary—that some connections would fall through the cracks or be deemed irrelevant. And the challenges to service learning do not reside exclusively within the university. My story continues.

Nonprofits and local community organizations themselves are complex and contradictory sites, and the mission of a nonprofit organization is seldom singular or uncontested. The stated mission of the street paper where I worked was "to empower the homeless or those at risk of becoming homeless to self sufficiency." *Empowerment* was the vague concept that structured the mission of the organization, and defining that term became a site of struggle and contradictions, sometimes explicitly but mostly in unacknowledged ways. Empowerment was defined in various ways: the director touted street papers as an entrepreneurial endeavor; social workers focused on personal development; the editorial staff invoked leftist critique to advocate community activism; I struggled to define what role education could play in "empowerment."[2]

These differences were not merely personal beliefs but were rooted in material and ideological concerns via grants and donations from business, religious, public health, and journalistic funding sources. The entrepreneurial director often criticized—and occasionally fired—editorial staff for being too political, yet invoked the paper's alternative news coverage in grants to media foundations. While we were in the business of helping people, none of us were ever allowed to forget that it was a business. Conflicts over mission were rarely articulated explicitly, but were experienced in day-to-day frustrations and disagreements with the director. I recognized these conflicts but tried not to focus on them and to get on with the work.

Then two ideas happened together: my own idea for a service-learning course and the Not Your Mama's Bus Tour (see Chapter 2). I decided that a nonfiction writing course at my university was the right size and skill level to write profile pieces (of vendors, volunteers, board members) for the newspaper's annual anniversary issue. The paper would get needed editorial content. Students would get interviewing, writing, and editing experience—and get published. A win-win situation.[3] I had learned from my earlier experiences and was going to do this the right way.

Over the next few months, two more things happened: I received a university fellowship and I got fired from the organization (well, I resigned but would have been fired if I hadn't). The fellowship allowed me to finish writing my dissertation and not to teach for one year while working at the nonprofit. But that meant that I wouldn't be teaching the service-learning course I had designed. Luckily, I found another grad student teaching the same course who was interested in doing the project. We started working together, planning and scheduling.

Then the bus tour hit the road. What a whirlwind. What a success. The publicity, the crowds, and the response were overwhelmingly positive, especially for the street-paper vendors who were the writers and performers. They were stars. I wouldn't trade those days for anything.

The more ambitious the bus tour grew, however, the more conflict I experienced with the nonprofit's director. Even though the project was running smoothly, I developed it as a public arts project that would break even financially, with a goal of public education and providing a livable-wage, temporary job to the vendors; the director envisioned a money-maker for the organization. Despite the director's pleasure in the project, the fact that it happened without his influence was a big problem. In the tense weeks leading up to the actual bus tours, my boss and I recognized that our productive three-plus-year working relationship was coming to an end. The day after the tour closed, I packed up my office.

I still wanted the service-learning course to be a success and did all I could to shepherd it along in absentia. My abilities were limited. Some students in the class attended the bus tour, were excited by it, and were then confused when they came to the office and found the Center locked during the first few weeks after my departure. Vendors who were no longer in the Center at regular times became hard to contact for interviews. Conflicting opinions about my departure made some people hesitant to talk. Busy board members were slow to return calls to an unknown person. There was a strange, awkward tension, but students didn't know the details and experienced only its effects. They were being asked to write about and publicly represent a complex and conflicted organization that they didn't understand. Unwittingly, depending on whom they interviewed, the students were weighing in on a conflicted situation where there was no neutral response. Articles ended up emphasizing the organization's director, board, and a few allied vendors, not the editorial staff or members of the writers' group. The students' projects were completed, but barely, and with much frustration. The teacher often called me, confused, and I ended up leaving messages for the editor. I felt bad for those students and can only imagine that they walked away from this project feeling ambivalent about the experience.

At this point, you might have more objections: "This is a personal conflict; there's no lesson to be learned here. If anything, your example shows why service-learning needs to be institutionalized and broadened, to allow it to claim enough institutional space so it can choose large and stable organizations with which to partner."

The situations I have recounted were not simply the result of bad luck, careless people, or an inability to follow rules. To personalize situations like these would erase the more important structural lessons they offer. Combining the complex and conflicted missions that underscore the daily life of nonprofits with an often-expanding university mission of service learning makes conditions ripe for disputes and allows connections to be missed, broken, or made in haphazard manners.

As I discuss later in this chapter, institutionalized service learning does allow for *certain* kinds of stability, continuity, and financial support. But at the same time, institutionalized service learning can't solve some problems, and even creates others; those in the communities we purport to serve are the ones who frequently experience these problems. My desire is to complicate the way we assess sending students into the streets by foregrounding the needs and responses of those in the communities served. What I argue is that while much of the recent scholarship in service learning has gained in complexity and sophistication over recent years, it still tends to prioritize student and institutional needs over community needs. This tendency correlates with a trend toward top-down institutionalization of service programs, promoted by organizations such as Campus Compact. Top-down service-learning programs frequently originate inside the university first and then seek out community sites of service. This runs the risk of framing local communities as generic sites of need, eager to benefit from university largess. The reality is that much of this service isn't as beneficial as some would like to think. By sharing additional examples of "service-learning-gone wrong" from the point of view of those who have been served, I seek to convey the frustration that some local partners feel about service connections that benefit students more than the community.

In response to what I see as a problematic development of top-down service programs, I propose an alternative model for creating community-university projects that are tactical, localized, and begin from developed relationships within communities. Rather than starting from institutional imperatives, tactical projects foreground the needs and expertise of communities, and seek to highlight—and work within—the possibilities and limitations inherent in university partnerships.

Service-Learning Scholarships: Good, in Principle

As an extension of the trend that asks students to engage in public writing and study local issues in the classroom, students are increasingly being sent into the streets as part of their education, through initiatives operating under a variety of terms, including *service learning*, *community internships*, and *experiential-based learning*. Service learning has become a large and visible aspect of a public turn, not just in writing studies, but across various disciplines and institutions, including universities, colleges, community colleges, and high schools. Advocates of service learning see courses in which students are connected in various ways to local communities as offering vital new ways for motivating students, reinvigorating composition curricula, and "rearticulat[ing] the university as part of, not opposed to, local communities" (Adler-Kassner et al. 1997, 4). Within composition studies, the turn toward service learning has been thoroughly documented and theorized. Tom Deans, in *Writing Partnerships*, a book-length study of the various initiatives grouped under the banner of service learning in composition, categorizes service projects as asking students to either write about, write for, or write with local communities.

Service learning has begun to claim strategic institutional spaces over recent years, in part through scholarship that has touted its success in offering active ways to "enrich the goals of a college composition classroom" (Duffy 2003, 5), "improve students' attitudes toward civic engagement and social responsibility . . . while enabling [them] to meet traditional standards for proficiency in the composition course" (Kendrick and Suarez 2003, 37), allow students to gain "positive literate experiences" (Martin 2000, 14), and solve classroom dilemmas, such as "empty assignment syndrome" (Brack and Hall 1997, 143) and "unreal rhetorical situations" (Heilker 1997, 71). This trend of optimism in early scholarship on service learning is not surprising, as Lillian Bridwell-Bowles (1997) writes: "With any new initiative in higher education, we typically find essays that contain individual testimonials from those who have tried the innovation, found it exciting, and hope to attract others" (22). Quickly, however, other scholars have added critical analyses to such optimistic rhetoric and have been writing about service learning in more complex ways, seeking to interrogate issues and problems. In a definitional essay on service learning, for example, Laura Julier (2001) raises many important concerns:

> Service learning pedagogy can seem . . . like a panacea, a gospel to be spread, a silver bullet that will energize and invigorate teachers, motivate students, connect academic activities with "real world" learning, and effect social change. Many of the reasons for excitement about service learning offered in those articles and conference sessions skim tired old surfaces even if with the enthusiasm of the newly converted. . . . Likewise there is often too little attention paid to questioning or problematizing the service activities and writing requirements, inquiring into and reconstituting, for instance, the idea of service, or what is meant by community and whose community, or how course assignments construct students and academic purposes in relationship to communities. (137)

These analyses, which could be considered a "second wave" of service-learning scholarship, problematize service learning in a variety of ways. Into what had been a predominance of success narratives has come a series of narratives that seek to take on the complexities of service learning, beginning in moments that were not as successful or invigorating as teachers would have hoped.[4] Such essays define the problems of and solutions to service learning in a variety of ways, ranging from the need for more critical reflection on the part of students[5] to the need for community groups to listen more to the advice of students.[6]

Nora Bacon's article "Community Service Writing" (1997) focuses on her service course in which students write for local nonprofits and community groups. She describes her own need to learn more about the writing demands of an unfamiliar institutional setting, and the challenge of asking students to write about ideas with which they might disagree. Caryn Chaden, Roger Graves, David A. Jolliffe, and Peter Vandenberg, in "Confronting Clashing Discourses: Writing the Space Between Classrooms and Community in Service-Learning Courses," argue that because service-learning students must confront the "clash" between discourses of the academy and those of community-based organizations, a service-learning course should help students address the challenge of negotiating these competing discourses (2002). Ellen Cushman's article "Sustainable Service Learning" (2002b) critiques short-sighted service courses and encourages faculty to conduct long-term research in service organizations. Other problems raised in critical service-learning scholarship include the need for students to understand broad public issues and forces,[7] to examine white, middle-class privilege,[8] and to understand and interrogate competing discourses and values.[9]

Another development in service-learning scholarship has been broadening efforts to theorize service learning and to widen the range of theoretical sources and models. Tom Deans (200b) credits the influences of John Dewey and Paulo Freire on service learning pedagogies. He shows how these two landmark educators influenced theoretical rationales for bringing students outside the classroom and into experiential interactions with local communities. The work of both Dewey and Freire emphasizes the connection between reflection and action, offering "a powerful vision of hope" (51). Dewey's goals are often pragmatic, with an eye toward reformation of existing democratic structures, while Freire's aims are more utopian and revolutionary. Deans describes some existing service-learning programs, which predominantly adopt the Deweyan pragmatic view of experience, as opposed to Freire's oppositional or revolutionary work.

Linda Flower credits the theories of Dewey and Cornel West in helping her develop a practice of "intercultural inquiry" in the Carnegie Mellon Community Literacy Center (Flower 2003; Flower et al. 2000) Margaret Himley (2004) relies on theories from feminist ethnography and postcolonial feminist theory to problematize the specter of "the other" that underlies service learning. Nancy Welch (2002) argues that psychoanalytic theory helps her and her students understand the complex interplay of subjectivities that takes place between server and served. Todd Harper, Emily Donnelli, and Frank Farmer (2003) argue for a more fully theorized understanding of service learning that will benefit from multiple metaphors and multiple theoretical perspectives regarding power and intersubjectivity. They move beyond pragmatist theories by drawing on three different theoretical "experiments" because, they argue, "We need to theorize service-learning because we need a specifically historical sense of our

practices, and how those practices are encompassed by larger structures and agendas" (636).

Critical scholarship helps make service learning a more complex
and thoughtful enterprise, with dedicated and knowledgeable instructors raising important concerns that should trouble all teachers. Lorie
Goodman's article "Just Serving/Just Writing" (1998) raises problems
related to service grounded in persistent questions: Why are we here?
What are we doing? Her cautionary words bear repeating:

> When we shift the scene of composition instruction beyond the walls
> of the academy and into "the community," we move beyond the
> realm of our own expertise and beyond the safety of our isolation.
> Our actions have consequences. Our grounds for action must remain
> under revision. We can never suppose that we are "just" serving; we
> must always ask, "In the service of what and whom?" (69)

The stakes of public work are broader than classroom concerns. As
such, our means for evaluating this kind of public work should go
beyond traditional markers of student achievement and evaluation. A
problem that persists throughout much service-learning scholarship,
however, is a continued reliance on traditional methods for evaluating
programs, which center on students. The student, his or her achievement, and his or her evaluations of the experience remain the primary
benchmark for the majority of individuals evaluating service-learning
projects. Flower, for example, notes that of 29 studies of service learning reviewed by Bacon and Dean, "the agenda, the assumptions and
the interpretations of community partners is rarely recognized as a
goal" (2002, 184).

When scholarship does recognize the agendas and assumptions of
community partners, it often does so in surface ways. Sometimes the
satisfaction of community partners is asserted as a bromide absent any
evidence, such as claiming that a community program "appreciated the
steadfast presence of college students in its tutoring sessions" (Bennet
2000, 20). Or else success is determined by how things appeared: "The
tutoring, as best we could determine, appeared to be productive for
learners at the shelter" (Herzberg 1994, 316). Notable exceptions
include Cushman (2002b) and Theresa Redd (2003), who emphasize
the need for long-term partnerships (Cushman) and deeper understandings of the rhetorical needs of organizations (Redd) for making
partnerships stronger.

Even some of the best work advocating a greater voice for community partners remains rooted in student concerns, while voices from
the street remain secondary. For example, in "Intercultural Inquiry and
the Transformation of Service," Linda Flower (Flower et al. 2000)
describes a seven-week program in which Carnegie Mellon University

(CMU) students and mostly African American teens from Pittsburgh discuss and write about an "urban issue" in connection with CMU's Community Literacy Center (189). "Collaborative intercultural inquiry," the idea underlying this project, invites CMU students to develop an inquiry about an urban issue grounded in their "troubling sense of contradiction telling [them] there was a more complex reality to grasp" (188). For example, Flower writes that CMU student Scott formed an inquiry into what has helped black male youths "form their own notion of work ethic" (189). He then invited teen students and other members of the community to develop a range of "rivaling" hypotheses and ideas about this issue. While this approach does put the ideas and wisdom of the community squarely into the project, the starting point for the inquiries remains the individual student and his assumptions. It's unclear to what extent the participating teens want to discuss issues of work ethics with a college student or if the inquiry benefited them in any way.[10]

In "Principles of Good Practice in Service-Learning," Suzanné Mintz and Garry Heisser (1996) admit that the practice of service learning doesn't always live up to its principles, that a "chasm exists between the development of principles and the success achieved in their application through practice" (30–1). In their list of the "critical elements of thoughtful community service"—community voice, orientation and training, meaningful action, reflection, and evaluation—evaluation, especially in ways that involve the community, is often neglected. Mintz and Heisser note that in 1995, only 20 percent of the members of the Campus Outreach Opportunity League (discussed in the next section) were implementing the recommended elements well (31). Gugerty and Swezey (1996) confirm this by reporting that seeking out information from the point of view of local communities is "the weak link" in the evaluation of most service programs (106). Other writers openly admit that service learning is designed to benefit students more than community groups: "The fact that service experiences are more likely to transform and enlighten the student than the community is not a reason for abandoning this work" (Hessler 2000, 36).

To summarize: On one hand, service learning has an increasingly sophisticated body of scholarship that includes researching programs and principles of service learning, problematizing the challenges of combining outreach and classroom learning, and theorizing outreach programs through an eclectic body of intellectual work. While the scholarship on service has gotten more critical and self-reflexive, local communities and their evaluation of this work remain secondary, appearing primarily in peripheral ways in the scholarship and evaluations of service-learning programs. One reason for this, I would argue, stems from how and why service learning has developed within colleges and universities.

The Promise and Perils of Institutionalized Service Learning

Even though many scholars connect service learning to past educational initiatives founded by educators like John Dewey[11] or Jane Addams[12] or point to the early use of the term *service learning* in the 1950s,[13] and even though the roots of service learning can be traced to countless grassroots projects developed by dedicated teachers and students,[14] the contemporary push toward institutionalized programs of service learning can be dated to the selfish decade of the 1980s and was born, in part, from public relations concerns. Patricia Hutchinson (2002) notes that "a desire for college students to challenge the common perception that young adults were self-seeking and out of touch with social issues" led to the development of the Campus Outreach Opportunity League (COOL) by a Harvard graduate in 1984. A year later, the presidents of Brown University, Georgetown University, and Stanford University founded Campus Compact to counter public images of college students as "materialistic and self-absorbed, more interested in making money than in helping their neighbors" by identifying service learning as a primary strategy for advancing a more positive image of college students (Campus Compact 2004a). H. Brooke Hessler (2000) asserts that desires for publicity and marketing continue to underscore many universities' interest in service learning:

> At a time when many colleges and universities are vying to differentiate themselves from competing institutions, it is no coincidence that service-learning programs are gaining administrative attention. Service learning represents a way to demonstrate institutional generosity and historical ties with the local community, presumably in contrast with the soul-less online and proprietary enterprises. (28)

In other words, service learning is, in the eyes of many academic administrators, an important marketing tool, a "unique selling point" for the institution.

Interestingly, however, service learning is becoming less unique and more the norm in higher education. As of 2004, Campus Compact lists as members the presidents of more than 900 two- and four-year private and public colleges and universities in 46 states and the District of Columbia. The conferences and publications of Campus Compact are funded by large corporations and foundations like General Electric, the

Ford Foundation, the Johnson Foundation, and the Corporation for
National Service (Campus Compact; Campus Compact "Wingspread").
Campus Compact supports the development of service learning through
a variety of initiatives: by promoting the growth of service learning on
member campuses (through the creation of guidelines, rubric, and syl-
labi); by creating campaigns that support the passage of federal legislation
promoting community service; by forming partnerships with business,
community, and government leaders; by organizing conferences and
meetings that provide information to members; and by awarding grants
and awards to member schools (Campus Compact 2004a).

Without drawing quick or simple conclusions, I think it's worth
asking some hard questions about the value of the rapid expansion of
service-learning programs fueled by organizations like Campus Compact. What difference does it make that such organized and well-
funded support for service learning has its roots in elite institutions and
is being promoted in a top-down model through a network of college
presidents? What difference does it make that the motivation to create
both the Campus Compact and COOL networks was grounded in a
desire for better public relations for ivy-league college students? What
models of service learning do national organizations promote? What
needs get prioritized and what concerns receive little attention?

In today's colleges and universities, the trend seems to be toward
creating long-term, top-down, institutionalized service-learning programs; or to continue with Michel de Certeau's terminology, universities privilege *strategic* rather than *tactical* service programs (1984).[15]
Strategies, according to de Certeau, seek to create stable spaces that can
overcome temporal changes. Creating strategies means institutionalizing, creating official spaces, like service-learning offices or university-
controlled community centers in local neighborhoods. As de Certeau
shows, seeking and creating strategic power has certain benefits:
Actions can be calculated, continuity can be assured, and broader
spaces can be claimed or controlled.

Clearly, predictability, continuity, and funded positions and spaces
can benefit service-learning programs a great deal. Scholars like Linda
Flower (2003) and Ellen Cushman (2002b, 2002a) make compelling
cases for the advantages that institutionalized and long-term service-
learning projects can yield. My concern, however, is that we must also
consider the disadvantages of institutionalized models and consider
more local *tactical* options as well.

Much scholarship related to service learning equates institutionalization with success. Statements such as these are commonplace: "The
success of service learning will depend on the level of its institutionalization and how the faculty accepts, adopts, and implements it within

the university" (Scapansky 2004); ". . . to foster the institutionalization of service learning . . . gives service learning advocates an ongoing voice in CCCC" (Deans 2000a); "Institutionalizing service-learning can be a critical strategy for mobilizing students as agents of social change who will also serve as positive representatives of higher education" (Hessler 2000). "In other words, service learning must become institutionalized within higher education" (Hutchinson 2002).

Campus Compact produces a variety of reports and documents encouraging institutionalization, including an annually updated report entitled *The Self-Assessment Rubric for the Institutionalization of Service-Learning in Higher Education*. This multivariable rubric is "designed to assist members of the higher education community in gauging the progress of their campus's service-learning institutionalization efforts" (Furco 2003). In short, the prevailing tenor of the discussion of institutionalizing service-learning programs frequently begs the question of the value of institutionalization, by assuming it as a natural and important goal.

In contrast, little scholarship raises critical questions about the value of creating institutionalized service projects. Margaret Himley (2004) does raise difficult ethical problems related to service learning, by placing fundamental questions about the shape and direction of service learning at the center of her inquiry:

> . . . [F]aced with so many dilemmas, I want to ask, what should we do as community service learning teachers? Institutionalize long-term relationships with agencies in the community (Flower; Heissler)? Become public intellectuals who conduct research in the community as collaborative inquiry (Cushman "Sustainable")? Abolish student-based service-learning courses? Replace journals with well-defined methodologies such as case-studies and ethnographies and make service learning more explicitly like ethnography? Never have students write about the service experience (Herzberg, cited in Welch)? Always have students write about the service experience (Welch)? . . . Get rid of service learning in first-year composition? Get rid of it altogether? (432–33)

Himley's openness both to questioning the foundations of service learning itself and to considering a range of options—of which institutionalization is only one—promotes a useful willingness to remain open to a variety of possible service models, or to move away from service if certain troubling problems can't be resolved.

A fairly direct critique of top-down institutionalized service programs is articulated by Bruce Herzberg in an interview with Tom Deans, in which he expresses concern "about the shift from grassroots to top-down implementation" in service learning:

I have encountered more and more people who said that they are being forced to implement service learning. The shift began at the close of the 1990s, I think. In the 1980s to early to mid-nineties, implementation was only made possible through huge and often self-sacrificing efforts by individual faculty members who believed in and were excited by community-based work. . . . So it's ironic that by the end of the 1990s we are in a situation where "the provost told me to do service learning." That's what I hear in workshops: "The dean mandated it"; "I was chosen to head up the project"; "I don't know anything about it, and I'm here to find out." And "I have to do assessment." And "I have no idea about what my budget is or how I'm supposed to promote this." And "There's a student requirement that they have to do service learning.". . . I haven't seen much written about this problem and I'm concerned that our community address this issue forcefully." (Deans 2002a, 75)

As Herzberg's comments suggest, service-learning programs that began because of the "huge and often-self sacrificing efforts" of individual instructors are being supplanted in many cases by top-down institutionalized efforts. To be fair, upper-level administrative support of service-learning programs can benefit existing service programs by sanctioning academic and staff time for the cultivation of service projects, establishing longer-term connections with community, and building in institutional rewards for faculty and staff engaged in service programs. An institutionalized service program can often claim measurable successes, be visible, and replicable.

While institutionalization of service learning is not evil on its face, it is risky and not necessarily beneficial, especially when universities institutionalize well-intentioned but top-down relationships. The very advantages of institutionalized service learning—measurable success, broad institutional presence, and sustainability—create a generic set of needs and priorities that make it difficult to respond to communities' needs and ideas. Rather than advocating institutionalization of service learning per se, we should ask, what values are we institutionalizing? What needs are we prioritizing? What risks do we incur when we seek to create broad, measurable, sustainable programs that claim institutional resources and space?

Harper, Donnelli, and Farmer (2003) warn that "institutions of higher learning risk becoming benevolent tyrants who injure the community by trying to save it." They describe the transition from "small independent service-learning projects into large administrative programs" in which "the institution is enriched through something of a colonizing enterprise, no matter how well intentioned such an enterprise may seem to individual students, teachers and administrators." A partnership becomes exploitative, they claim, when power is viewed as "unidirectional, flowing from a root source to its branches" creating a sense of the university that "gains a greater understanding of itself as it interacts, appropriates and projects itself onto the other" (619).

In seeking sustainability of strategic service programs, we need to critically examine the kinds of projects or relationships we are seeking to inscribe and repeat. The very need to repeat service projects in many different course sections, semester after semester, may predetermine what kinds of projects are created. To decide a year ahead, for example, what needs several hundred college students can fulfill in a limited amount of time, determined by the academic schedule, makes it more likely that the projects will be somewhat generic and not responsive to the particular rhetorical moment. Strategic planning, by definition, means securing stable continuity over time, and in many ways resists local rhetorical responsiveness. When service learning is a predetermined goal, *kairos*, or timeliness is sought—if at all—only after a decision is made that students must find some service to perform. When a program prioritizes continuity, it risks solving the difficult task of finding service sites for students semester after semester by relying on models that define service as a generic and benign task—like tutoring or serving a meal at a soup kitchen. Such models proceed from a problem approach, in which the community is defined as the source of the problem, which the university defines and on whose behalf the students work.

Finally, when seeking to promote top-down, ongoing service-learning programs, one risks glossing over or overlooking the real limitations of time and of the projects themselves. The people we work with in the streets don't live or think in terms of semesters or quarters or finals or spring breaks. The rhythms of the university do not necessarily harmonize with the rhythms and exigencies of community groups. If the impetus driving service learning is a desire to promote the university as a site of good work, how likely is it that universities will do multiple, meaningful service projects semester after semester, classroom after classroom, in exactly the amount of time a semester allows? As the following examples show, it is not very likely.

Too-Common Examples?

What would happen to our theorizing and principles about service learning if we listened to the community more? How effectively are top-down programs "serving" our partners? I asked some nonprofit workers and community friends around the United States and in the United Kingdom to talk to me about their experiences of working with university students. Sadly, it was easy to gather the following stories.

Example 1: What the Student Wants

The following email was sent to the offices of *Spare Change News*, Boston's street newspaper, on January 29, 2003:

> Hi,
>
> My name is April[16] ____ and I am a senior at ____ University. I am currently in a writing course and have been assigned your organization as my client for the semester. Through this course, I must produce various assignments that involve media proposals/campaigns to educate people about *Spare Change* and homelessness. I was wondering if it would be possible for you to send me any information your organization has, i.e. flyers, brochures, organizational material, etc, that you have in your office (that are unavailable online)? Even better, would it be possible for me to come in and meet with someone to talk about your organization so I can better understand how to represent you? Or attend any meetings you have scheduled? When you have the opportunity, please get back to me.
>
> Thank you,
>
> April ____

I ran across April's email as part of my regular volunteer editorial work at *Spare Change*, having been asked by the editor to go through the email and sort out the important pieces. I printed it out and brought it to Fran Czajkowski, executive director of the organization. She read it, laughed, and threw it aside, saying, "No thanks. Help like that is no help at all."

April may have been surprised that her email never received a reply. She might have felt frustrated or angry that her classwork became more difficult than she had hoped, since she did not get the meeting she requested. She might have even felt resentful that a course required her to offer what she considered help to the homeless and no one ever got back to her. Her teacher might even write someday about the difficulty of getting service organizations to cooperate.[17] This was clearly not a successful community-university partnership.

More than just a stray example, this story exemplifies the problems that can occur when teachers themselves are not connected to the community and *assign* organizations to students or ask students to *seek out* sites themselves. I think it's useful to interrogate why the nonprofit saw this as an undesirable offer and imagine how April's teachers could have set up a more successful experience.

When I interviewed Fran about the situation, she remarked that the student's email announced that she was assigned this nonprofit for the semester yet she had no information about the paper. This was, as all staff confirmed, the first contact anyone in the organization had received from anyone at April's university relating to this course. Who was the instructor who *assigned* April this organization? What responsibilities did he or she have to that organization when it became required course content? April's email indicated that she *must* produce media proposals/campaigns to educate *people* about this local nonprofit and homelessness. Whether or not such documents would be useful to this organization seems not to have been considered at all.

April's request represents not only a logistical failing but a rhetorical one as well. Throughout her email, April wrote only about *her* needs and what *she* must do for *her* class. She expressed that she couldn't find the information she needed on the Web and made three requests of the organization, two which would be time consuming (send documents and meet with her), and a third that seems inappropriate altogether: to allow the student to attend internal meetings. Fran remarked that this third request seemed surprisingly forward and was typical of other students' attitudes toward community nonprofits. "Could you imagine a student making the same request of IBM or even a local tax agency? It wouldn't happen," she said (Czajkowski 2003).

Fran also expressed frustration because the student could have learned more about the organization prior to contacting her. Street newspapers are sold on the streets by vendors who are homeless or low-income; their pages provide information about homelessness and the organizations themselves. So, for a dollar, April could have better prepared herself before contacting *Spare Change*.

In addition to lacking a rhetorical sense of her audience, April's email also lacked *kairos* or a sense of timeliness, in terms of what was currently going on in the organization. If she had read the paper, she would have learned that the development committee at *Spare Change* had been cultivating a relationship with a local advertising agency to develop a public-awareness campaign, which would be hitting the streets around the time she sent the email. Such campaigns take a great deal of time and expertise to develop and implement, more than one semester's work from one undergraduate student. April herself offered nothing to the organization in exchange for her requests. She did not even try to make the case that her assignment might be useful to the organization.

In one sense, April's teacher put April in a difficult and a rhetorical situation, requiring her to create documents for an organization with no sense of its current needs, just a generic imperative to *help*. Along with this imperative, the instructor granted the students at least the hypothetical right to publicly represent a community organization. Fran was surprised that April was asked by her instructor—and seemed comfortable claiming—this right without knowing the organization or even asking their consent.

In a perfect world, small nonprofits like *Spare Change News* would have enough staff to keep their website fully up to date and to reply to even unhelpful requests like April's. The very fact that they can't shows that nonprofits often lack the material resources that would make quick and easy "student service" useful. Fran describes the situation this way:

> It's often more work to explain what we need to a class of unprepared students than to do it ourselves. Especially when students are just interested in us because of one course or one project, it's not worth our time. I get about 30 phone calls each semester from college students wanting to do final projects for some course or another on *Spare Change* and they all want to meet with me, and I just say no. Even when teachers try to set it up, they approach me as a stranger. They often know so little about our organization or our needs that the time required makes it not worth it. Plus as an organization, we've been burned too many times by promises. (Czajkowski 2003)

Fran's remarks attest to problems that result when partnerships are not grounded in ongoing local relationships, and connections with local organizations occur after a service-learning course is designed. Courses that ask students to choose sites of service not only risk framing service as a generic good, they also risk providing a disservice to community partners.

Example 2: Burn Me Twice—Master's Student Doesn't Deliver

Fran mentioned being "burned" by other university partnerships, and when I asked her to explain, she easily found examples. She described a project that seemed carefully planned to have a reciprocal and positive outcome for all involved. A graduate student in communications and her advisor contacted the organization, hoping to produce a documentary video about the newspaper and its vendors. The student planned the project as her master's thesis and the organization would receive a professionally made video about itself. The professor promised that *Spare Change* would have a say in determining the length, angle, and participants in the video. The student promised to stay out of the way and to be a minimal intrusion on the organization. Fran agreed to give the student access to staff, vendors, volunteers, meetings, and upcoming events. Based on all principles of community partnerships, the planning seemed sound.

In reality, the project required much more time of staff, vendors, and volunteers than originally proposed. "That was all right, though," Fran said. "We were hoping for a video we could really use." Some months after the filming ended, Fran received an email indicating that the video was complete; the thesis project had been passed. She was assured that "after a few final edits" the organization's video would arrive.

As of this writing, more than two years after the video was promised to the organization, nothing has arrived. Repeated efforts to contact the student and her advisor have resulted in promises but no video; the student received her master's thesis but the organization received no film.

When instructors set up projects that advocate "writing for the community" (Deans), how careful and sure are we that the final work arrives and is assessed by the organization? Once grades are handed in and we move on to the next semester or project, how carefully do we follow up to be sure the student work has met a specific need?

Example 3: No One Burned, But No One Helped Much Either

A business writing faculty member approached a large street paper and asked if her students could develop new project ideas and write up marketing proposals for the publication. Lisa, one of the paper's staff members, made herself available to answer questions from students and the faculty member; she offered to visit the class to discuss the publication and its current projects. After the term ended, the instructor arrived carrying a box filled with glossy-covered reports, recommending a variety of projects for the publication. After the instructor left, I asked the staff member, "What will you do with all of those?"

"Honestly," she replied, "Probably not much. I'll glance through them, but there's probably not much here that will be of use to us."

I then asked about the instructor. Lisa said, "The instructor is a very nice woman. Spoke to me a few times. But in the course of a few conversations, it was hard to imagine what kind of projects students could do that would also be directly relevant to us in one term. We've met this faculty member, but she didn't know our organization all that well. None of these student projects will be specific enough to really meet any of our needs."

Finally, I inquired as to what might have made this connection more useful. Lisa said, "I'm not sure, because I don't know the needs and requirements of the class very well. Maybe if [the faculty member] had spent some time, even doing some volunteer work, she could have suggested more specific projects. Or even better, it might be interesting to plan a class together."

The good news of this example is that the teacher did speak with the organization before the semester. She did follow through. She drove with a box of reports to the community organization, and she honestly hoped they would be useful. The course was set up, however, to teach students to write marketing proposals. The assessment of the course did not include attention to whether or how the proposals were useful or timely in the eyes of the organization.

As I'll discuss near the end of this chapter, establishing another model of community partnerships might mean taking the partnership idea even more seriously. Specific courses could then be planned around specific needs of specific groups at specific times.

Example 4: The Case of the Vanishing Intern

A midwestern university's internship office arranged a required undergraduate service internship for a student to spend a summer working 20 hours a week for an East Coast nonprofit that had a paid staff of four. Megan Mahoney, one of the staff members, spoke with the internship advisor, exchanged emails with the student, and made plans for his arrival. Megan spent much of the first day with him, teaching him about the organization, offering different projects or areas where he could work, and getting him set up on the computer system. On his next scheduled day in the office, he did not arrive or call. Concerned phone calls and emails to both the student and the faculty advisor weren't returned. He never returned for a second day of work.

More than two weeks later, an email arrived at the organization that read, in its entirety, as follows:

Hi, It's [first name].

Please tell [staff member] and whoever else needs to know that I can't volunteer for you anymore. I'm sorry that I didn't tell you this beforehand, and I'm sorry if there are complications. I can explain this at some other time.

Thank you.

[first and last name]

After Megan forwarded me this email, I asked her about the experience, including how much time was lost. "It could have been worse," she said. "He was only in the office for a day." Since he had committed to 20 hours per week, however, the organization had planned for him to pick up slack left by the prolonged illness of a part-time staff member. Because of his abrupt withdrawal and the two-week gap before telling them he wouldn't return, the organization had to scramble to fill the holes.

I asked if she would be willing to partner with this university again. "I'd be reluctant," she said.

When universities require service of students—in the form of mandatory service-learning classes or internship—the service opportunity is designed to offer the student a specific kind of experience. At the same time, however, such a requirement displaces the responsibility of educating college students on community organizations not compensated for, and often inconvenienced by, such work.

Example 5: The Tutee Talks Back

Charles Ferguson, a *Spare Change News* vendor, has "been served" by students at several Boston-area shelters and service organization. He told me that, like many people he knows, he has grown wary of students and sometimes even deceives them:

> Sometimes college students come into the neighborhood or the shelter for a class. They're just putting in their time or collecting their information, and that's it. They want to have an experience with me quick, write an essay, get in and get out. Study our behavior. Probably to laugh at you. There are plenty of writers. They want to exchange emails, get my phone number. As soon as they've got what they need, they're gone. I don't know if they think we notice, we do. People I know make up stories, lies, to tell them. They call it "game," something to do to pass time, to play back when someone is doing something to you. Recently, a [university] student from told me that he wanted to write a story on homeless people. I had a question for him, why should he get my story? (Ferguson 2004)

I asked Charles if he felt that the kind of troubles he experienced indicate that it would be better not to send students into places like shelters. He thought about it, and offered the following advice, underscoring a belief that all useful connections depend on why students are sent, for how long, and what they know about a neighborhood or community:

> What advice would I give? Be in no hurry, be cool. Spend some time. Don't show people you are so intense wanting something from them. Also, many of the students are white, and many of them have never been around too many black people. When white people are nervous around black people, we can tell. Don't just show up a few times, make a real commitment to a neighborhood, be part of it. (Ferguson 2004)

The scholarship in service learning has already addressed the need for service projects to be integrated into communities (Flowers), to attend to student attitudes (Herzberg; Schutz and Gere 1998; Green 2003) and to include long-term commitments by faculty (Cushman). One could argue that the examples I offer occurred only because someone merely did not keep up with current scholarship or follow the rules of accepted Campus Compact protocol[18] in working in service-learning contacts.

Yet I argue that the problem goes beyond individual mistakes. The gaps between theory and its practice should not be overlooked or glossed over but rather foregrounded as what Carrick, Himley, and Jacobi (2000) describe (borrowing from Paulo Freire) as *ruptura*, "conflict[s] that force us to make a decision, to act, to break away from the old and familiar" (57).

Even isolated cases of campus community work gone wrong cast long shadows for everyone involved in university-community partnerships. It takes just one experience of "being burned" for a community group to sour on the idea of working with our students. Especially in smaller communities, how many annoyed nonprofits will it take before universities have trouble finding "placements" to help educate their students? And even when partnerships run more smoothly—when the video does arrive or the marketing proposals do show up—how much do the projects really benefit the community groups? How good are we at asking and finding out? It is worth considering whether the costs to community groups justify the perceived benefits of top-down service programs that require sending students into the streets semester after semester.

A Case for Local, Tactical Community Projects

Given the powerful institutional needs, material supports, and a wide body of scholarship promoting institutionalized service learning,[19] it seems likely that such initiatives will grow or at least persist in the near future. Whether such *strategic* development of service learning in the long term is viable will depend on local and institutional relationships, antagonisms, personalities, and material supports. While I doubt this chapter will stem the tide toward broad, strategic service projects, I would like to take up Harper, Donnelli, and Farmer's call to "imagin[e] possible other futures for how service-learning might be manifest within and beyond institutions of higher learning" (2003, 636) by advocating localized, *tactical*, and carefully—if at all—institutionalized projects. These projects should develop and grow from the bottom up, not the top down, not mandate service of students, consider the community as a source of expertise, and acknowledge and seek to work rhetorically within the specificity and limitations of space and time. Before elaborating on these characteristics of *tactical projects*, I share one example.

One Tactical Project: Kids' 2 Cents

Before arriving at *Spare Change News* in the fall of 2001, I foolishly and incorrectly assumed that I might be able to "leverage" the time I had spent at the street paper in Chicago and move smoothly and quickly into engaged projects in Boston. After all, I knew street papers, plus I knew the Boston staff somewhat from annual street-paper conferences. When I traveled to Boston for my campus job interview, I spent one afternoon at the street-paper office talking over needs, projects, and ideas.

Once I relocated, however, I realized that, just like in Chicago, I needed to spend time keeping my mouth shut and doing whatever work needed doing before understanding the local setting well enough to help create anything new. For the first year, I made myself a general workhorse—mostly writing grants and news stories, copyediting, or doing other grunt editorial work. Fran, the organization's director, and I would talk about possibilities as I got to know—and to be known by—the vendors and staff of the paper. I learned that just because I was familiar with the work they did didn't mean they would be familiar or comfortable with me.

Occasionally Fran would mention an idea that interested her, a desire to help the roughly 9,000 readers of the fortnightly newspaper understand that, in Massachusetts, *homeless* is a term that often means children and families, even though most people you see on the streets are men; rarely one can identify homeless families on the streets. We talked about the values underlying a street paper, of wanting not merely to report *about* homeless children but to hear *from* them, to demystify the concept "homeless child" by embodying it with words, stories, and images. One night, Fran said, "I imagine a supplement to *Spare Change* called *Kids' 2 Cents*" (Czajkowski 2003). She said she knew an organization that worked with children in area shelters. I said, "This might be a project to connect my students with." The organization Fran spoke with recommended that we contact a shelter in Waltham, Massachusetts; Fran called the director and the three of us agreed to meet.

The shelter director told us that she read *Spare Change*, which is why she agreed to meet with us. At first she was gruff and skeptical, which I understood, but she said she liked the paper and heard good things about the organization. Even though I represented my university in that meeting, I was also a *Spare Change* trustee and volunteer. After a long discussion of rules, CORIs[20] and preparation, she agreed to let us test out weekly meetings of the Kids' 2 Cents Writing Group with the school-age kids living at the shelter, although she warned us that there might not be any interest.

I didn't want "service" to be mandatory in my fall-semester Literatures of Homelessness class (see Chapter 3). Once we got the approval from the shelter, I announced the Kids' 2 Cents project to the class as one possibility for the students' course project, asking interested people to see me. We ended up with a group of seven who signed on and attended an orientation held by the director, Fran, and me. None of us knew how well the weekly project would work. I told the students, "No one might want to work with us. The kids might not like the idea of a writing group or the idea of university kids coming to hang out with them. Whatever happens happens. Your grade will be determined by your participation in setting up and attending the project and your presentation to our class about the project—not by whether this project works. Failure or lack of continuation are both viable options." The freedom for the project not to succeed was important for me, and for the students. I didn't want us to find ourselves in a situation where we felt we *had* to make homeless kids work with us.

My students and I met before our first writing-group meeting, made books for each child to fill, and bought art supplies—gel pens, fruity-smelling erasers, paper bags, construction paper, even paint. We assembled some story and poetry books for reading aloud. We hoped for the best.

Our first evening, in October, we set up in a family meeting room in the shelter, which houses 38 families. Soon a stream of children came running in, and with simple questions like "Would you like to draw?" or "Want to write a story?" we had a writing group. During the twenty-minute ride to the shelter each week, our group would plan activities. On the way home we would review the evening and consider changes.

As the semester neared its end, we had barely talked with the kids about *Spare Change* or publishing their writing. We had mentioned it—to them and their moms—but in the weekly flurries of drawing, writing, and reading aloud, publishing hadn't taken center stage. While we had enough writing to assemble an issue of the paper, the timing seemed wrong.

I talked with the students, and they shared my apprehension. I said that whatever was completed by the end of the semester would be fine in my eyes in terms of grades. Their obligation to the course would end in December. But I also said, "I think I'd like to keep coming after break. To work a few more months and wait until the time feels right for publishing an issue of the paper. No one is required to keep coming. But, if anyone wants to, you're welcome."

Five of the seven students decided to keep coming to the writing group each week, along with the two English graduate students who had been helping from the beginning. Three more months of weekly visits after the semester ended, the time felt right. Kids were often asking about the publication of the newspaper. We typed up all of the writing and assembled artwork and photographs. The director read through the entire manuscript and the moms gave permission to publish each piece of their child's writing and a photograph. The kids' writing and images filled eight of the newspaper's sixteen pages. The rest of the paper was filled with articles completed by students in the Litera-tures of Homelessness class, contextualizing the issue of homelessness and families with articles about housing costs and state policies for schooling homeless kids, reviews of children's books about homeless-ness, and background pieces about the writing group itself. The issue was published at the end of March 2003 and sold out before the two-week run had finished.

At the end of the year, I had three meetings—with the students, the shelter director, and the staff at *Spare Change*—to discuss the pro-ject's successes and problems. All expressed a desire for the project to continue, but Literatures of Homelessness was not being offered the next year.

All of the groups decided to continue the project. The second year of Kids' 2 Cents took place absent a direct connection to a single course: Some students from the class continued our weekly visits, and some first-year writing students taught by the participating graduate students or me signed on too. Everyone involved agreed to attend the writing group and to write one article for the newspaper. We published another "Kids' 2 Cents" issue in the spring of 2004. At the time of this writing, another series of meetings is planned for all parties to decide if and how the project should continue.

I describe this project as *tactical* in that it originated not from uni-versity needs but from the articulated needs of one community group (*Spare Change*), and involved another community group as well as uni-versity students. The project was connected to a class with a topic specifically dedicated to issues of homelessness and writing. Asking homeless children to share their stories was an attempt to frame the community as a source of knowledge, not a source of deficit. The proj-ect was framed as an artistic project, encouraging kids to write, draw, take photos, and tell stories about whatever it was they wanted to write, draw, or tell about.[21] Since neither the course nor the project was defined by institutionalized service-learning structures, it could be adaptable in seeking to negotiate the timeframe between the univer-sity schedule and the organic needs of the project itself—the best way to build trust, continuity, and enough momentum. Continuity of the project is a question, not an imperative; the project will continue or not continue in the future, depending on the desires of all parties.

Tactical projects have their limitations as well as their strengths. For the children's writing group, the onus of organizing and logistics remained with me, the project director. I raised small amounts of cash from the university and through the street paper. After the first semes-ter, my car was the only vehicle to get students to the shelter. That meant I could never miss a week—and there were many Thursday nights when I had hoped or needed to do just that. In the second year, I lent my car on the nights I had a meeting conflict, and a few graduate students helped share the burden of organizing and driving. The street paper approved a small budget, but the students and I purchased all supplies and struggled to keep track of receipts in order to be reimbursed. In tactical projects, resources and efforts are highly localized. A more institutionalized program might have provided transportation and supplies and helped expand the program.

My question, though, has been and remains this: At what cost would institutionalization have helped this project? If Kids' 2 Cents were a larger, more institutionally sanctioned program, it likely could not have remained as flexible. If it became ongoing and expected, how quickly or easily could it decide to no longer publish the writing of children living in a shelter, if it seemed the newspaper or university were benefiting more than the children? How likely is it that an institutionalized version of this project would decide that a new project with the same kids—or no project at all—would be better . . . for now? And who would make that decision in an institutional program—an instructor, a service-learning coordinator, a dean? And what values or urgencies would get prioritized?

While much scholarship touts the value of institutionalizing projects, it is equally worth noting the value of creating local, tactical projects. Tactical projects view the community as a source of expertise, foreground specific community needs, involve students in work that has specific rhetorical exigencies, and acknowledge their own limitations. Individually, these characteristics can be found in many existing service-learning projects and could be adapted into more strategic initiatives.

Viewing the Community as a Source of Expertise

As I described in the Introduction, a project orientation, as opposed to a problem orientation, views the constituency—whether it be students or a local community group—as a source of knowledge and expertise. Tactical service-learning projects may be grounded in ongoing, pressing social concerns; but rather than adopting a problem approach that frames the community as a site of deficit or need, they seek ways to construct projects that acknowledge the expertise and capacity existing there.

Many examples of *writing for the community* and *writing with the community,* as outlined by Thomas Deans, construct partnerships that highlight the expertise of communities. Even more so would be projects that I would like to call *writing by the community*, which include projects that assist in community publishing and oral-history publishing (see, e.g., Owens 2001; Cassell; Goldblatt and Parks 2000) as well as a wide range of academic research exploring extracurricular literacy (such as

Gere 1994; Brandt 2001; Cushman 1998; Mathieu 2003; Powell and Takayoshi 2003). The value in all of this work is to create relationships that not only claim reciprocity in a general way, but create bodies of knowledge that undercut elitist notions that frame communities, especially in urban areas, as sites of problems that only academic experts can fix. Tactical projects prioritize an exchange of skills or ideas over ameliorating a problem.

Foregrounding Community in Project Creation and Assessment

In many service programs, projects or ideas initiate within the institution and extend outward. Teachers or administrators often decide, first, that service is a good idea, then seek connections to allow service to take place. Tactical projects begin or are grounded early on in locations outside the university or result from relationships that exist for other reasons than the research or service connection. While the goal of strategic programs is to be organized and efficient, tactical projects are anything but efficient. Efficiency might develop over time, if a specific project warrants efficiency, but the process itself is not methodical or specific. For example, a graduate student might decide to start volunteering with a local environmental organization because he or she cares about the work the organization does. He or she might hope that a service-learning connection might develop over time. It would only develop, however, if and when an appropriate match is made between local needs and the university classroom.

Ideas for tactical projects can generate inside or outside the university and can be fueled by students, teachers, or nonprofit staff. For example, an undergraduate at the University of Washington, Erin Anderson, worked as a volunteer at *Real Change News* and became excited about the possibilities of making greater connections between her university and the newspaper. She brokered an introduction between the paper's director and a faculty member, which led to continued meetings. Throughout it all, Erin served as an important liaison and source of information as future projects developed. The university approved a two-credit course, Street Papers, Poverty and Homelessness, which the nonprofit director taught as an adjunct faculty member and involved University of Washington students. Plans are underway to further develop this partnership throughout the street-paper network with a developing university global classrooms project.[22]

Understanding That Service/Activism Is Never Neutral

Tactical courses acknowledge that no act or deed is neutral and that any act of service promotes certain needs while undermining others.

Serving a cup of soup at a shelter provides immediate needs to a hungry person but does nothing to change the system that makes that person hungry in the first place. Lobbying for affordable housing seeks to change the system that makes people homeless, but does nothing to meet immediate needs. In a tactical view, all projects are incomplete.

One example of a service course that approaches decisions about service as value-laden is Peter Vandenberg's course on the rhetoric of graffiti at DePaul University (see Chaden et al. 2002). In this course, students study and photograph local graffiti and begin to understand it as a phenomenon over which people disagree. Students learn that the city wants to paint over all graffiti, including murals. Graffiti artists see their work as making important public statements. Community residents have varying opinions, designating some graffiti as worth preserving and other graffiti as gang tagging that needs to be covered over. The students in Vandenberg's course document all the graffiti that they find and study on a website, acknowledging its value and the need to archive it. Yet students also work with local community groups to help them either preserve or cover over specific graffiti. This might mean writing city officials regarding preservation permits or painting a sealant over a mural wall. On the other hand, it might mean whitewashing garage doors or painting spray-painted bricks. Either way, students realize that they are working in a contested space and honor the opinions of certain community members regarding the graffiti, well aware that others (including themselves) may feel differently about the decisions being made. In this example, students serve a limited and specific rhetorical function.

Using Space and Time Rhetorically

Whereas a strategic development of service learning seeks to create institutional spaces that sanction and allow for the development and sustainability of service projects, a tactical approach works within and learns from the belief that local streets and communities are not controlled by any university. Rather than seeking to control or institutionalize space, a tactical orientation privileges timeliness and sensitivity to space. As Michel de Certeau (1984) asserts, tactics are rhetorical acts that rely on and take advantage of opportunities that present themselves; one pins one's hopes not on control but on using time in clever ways (37–39). The limitations and artificiality of time, especially as it is doled out in a university setting, define the limits of all service-learning enterprises; in a tactical orientation, the radical insufficiency of the acts we perform is foregrounded, not as a critique of a project but as a necessary component of remaining accountable as teachers and students.

Any project will feel sand in its gears when the timeframes of daily life and university life meet. In the Kids' 2 Cents project, the college students need to keep to a schedule to allow themselves to include work with homeless children in a writing group each week. But to the children, our scheduled interaction includes large and often artificial gaps: missing weeks at Thanksgiving, spring break, Easter; a missing month in December; entire disappearances in the summer. Even though it was planned this way, even though the organization understands, and even when we explain to the kids why we'll be away and when we'll be back, there's pain there, or at least disruption, in the lives of kids who've already experienced profound disruptions. A tactical approach prompts me to think about and discuss this issue for next year: Are there ways to minimize the gaps, or try to make better plans with the shelter so our absences can correspond with other activities they schedule for the kids? While my students and I appreciate and benefit from the rhythms of a university's cycle, that cycle doesn't always fit with the rhythms of life in the streets outside of campus. Rather than merely accepting this disconnect, a tactical orientation seeks clever ways to work around such limitations—such as continuing projects beyond a semester—or at least to acknowledge the real limitations of time.

Acknowledgement can be as simple as rhetorical awareness. For example, when service-learning coordinators used to contact me at the street paper seeking "placements for next semester," I happened to know approximately when that might begin and for how long that would last. But the language of credit hours and semesters are not as meaningful as actual days, dates, number of weeks, or even fiscal years to some nonprofits. A tactical approach reminds us that the university does not control the turf, nor the discourse, and that learning to work in the streets requires such sensitivity and awareness.

Beyond Binaries: How Can Strategic Programs Act More Tactically?

In this chapter I have described service-learning projects along a spectrum ranging from strategic—focused on institutionalization and sustainability—to tactical—prioritizing bottom-up, time-contingent, flexible development of projects. Clearly, as I hope some of these examples show, this strategic-tactical binary serves a more rhetorical purpose rather than a descriptive one; approaches to doing neighborhood projects range from large top-down, mandatory, general service programs to extremely ad hoc unfunded labors of love that last for a short time and then disappear. By exploring the strategic-tactical binary, I hope to have made the case for the values inherent in more tactical projects: organic origins, a project orientation that frames the community as a source of knowledge, genuine community involvement in planning and evaluation, and a rhetorical sense of timeliness and the limitations of time.

Tactical projects are grounded in timeliness and hope and as such seek not measurable outcomes but completed projects. The projects have value in themselves but hope for intangible changes—in students, in community members, in the university itself. The key to that hope, however, is an acknowledgement of the radical insufficiency of any single project.

Such subjective and rhetorical values might not be practical or easy to implement within university administration. If universities are serious about walking the walk of "serving" the community and getting beyond public relations catchphrases, however, we need to find ways to make and keep community projects local, specific, responsive, and timely. Such a commitment may require forgoing institutionalized service-learning projects altogether or insisting that programs are only institutionalized from the bottom up, project by project, relationship by relationship. This kind of a commitment would also require significant questioning or redefining of the work of teachers, writers, and scholars in the university. In the concluding chapter, I turn to these questions.

Notes

1. See Deans 2000.
2. Many of these conflicts and complications are explored in my dissertation *Questions of Empowerment: Teaching Writing at a "Homeless" Community Newspaper*. Ph.D Dissertation. University of Illinois at Chicago 2001.
3. For a response to service-learning rhetoric of reciprocity, see Carrick, Hamler, and Jacobi.
4. E.g., Bacon; Duffy; Green; Sayer; Redd; Bennett; Herzberg 1994.
5. See Schutz and Gere; Herzberg (1994, 2000).
6. See Bennett.
7. See Schutz and Gere; Himley.
8. See Green.
9. See Chaden et al.; Welch; Himley.
10. The Carnegie Mellon Community Literacy Center does publish collaborative position papers developed by community and university participants through the work of its Community Think Tank. See http://www.cmu.edu/thinktank/thinktank4.html.

11. See Deans 2000b.

12. See Flowers 1997.

13. See Hutchison.

14. See Schutz and Gere; Deans 2000b; Zlotkowkski.

15. For a discussion of *strategies* and *tactics*, see Chapter 1.

16. The name has been changed but the rest of the content is not altered.

17. Some service-learning scholarship reports complaints by students or instructors about community groups either not returning calls or being resistant to suggestions by the students or faculty. See for example Cullum or Bennett.

18. See Campus Compact "Wingspread."

19. A recent Google search resulted in 3,720 hits for the phrase "institutionalized service learning"; adding "English" and "college" or "university" to the phrase still generated 1,520 hits. While not conclusive, this search shows that, at least on websites, there is a lot of discussion about institutionalized service learning, nearly none of which is critical of the trend.

20. Criminal Offender Record Information (CORI) is the name given to the standard criminal background check currently required for anyone wanting to work with children staying in state facilities.

21. We never asked students to write specifically about homelessness or the difficulties in their lives. The majority of the writing never touched on difficult issues, but was mostly about things like space aliens or dogs named Christina Aguilera. A few older kids did choose to write about life in a homeless shelter or about poor people in general. The mothers of each child read—or were read—every piece of writing, and we only printed work that they had approved.

22. For more information about the Global Classrooms Initiative, visit http://www.washington.edu/oue/faculty/globallearn.html.

Five

Teachers/Writers/Scholars in the Streets

Working with students and watching them grow through experiences has been rewarding. Working with college staff, professors, board members, etc. has been the difficult part. It seems that their interests lie in teaching a lesson to their students that they themselves don't yet understand.
—Jane, Homeless Outreach Worker

At the heart of designing, assigning, teaching, overseeing, researching, and cataloguing the initiatives that connect campuses with local streets and neighborhoods are academic professionals: teachers, scholars, and administrators. The turn to the streets within composition studies affects and implicates faculty directly involved in such work but also raises questions for the entire profession, about the roles, responsibilities, and limitations of academics involved in public work. Given that much of our scholarship calls us to be involved in various ways in the streets and communities outside of campus, we should examine the motivations for and the value of this work.

This concluding chapter asks questions about public-academic initiatives within English composition studies and argues that turning to the streets necessitates a serious re-examination of the work we do as teachers, writers, and scholars. Through an overview of recent scholarship, I suggest that public roles for writing faculty vary, including that of public intellectual, community researcher, and campus-community-program administrator. While the motivations for such work are often genuine, the disciplinary systems of assessment of academics can creative uneven or even exploitive partnerships. As an example, I share one final horror story—of a faculty-community partnership that left those in the streets feeling bitter.

To counter the dangerous tendency to use rather than help those in the streets, I advocate expanding the definition of public-academic work to include projects that utilize academic expertise not to further the immediate professional ends of the scholar but to meet the immediate needs and circulate knowledge in local communities. I illustrate this alternative role by exploring the grounded work of three academics—Sandra Andrews, Diana George, and Howard Zinn—that exemplifies ways to seek innovative and nonexploitive means of working within existing communities. In this way, I seek to sketch visions of locally engaged teachers/writers/scholars who use their rhetorical expertise to make contributions to local campaigns and ongoing communities grounded in tactics and hope, not in specific research or publishing agendas. A tactical model of scholarship necessitates being open to possibilities for redefining academic work beyond traditional categories of research, teaching, and service/administration. If scholars within English want to define their work lives to include concerns that transcend campus borders, such a desire necessitates more than good intentions or a bit of free time. It requires reworking or defying the strategic demands on our working lives in order to act on the tactical knowledge we gain in communities.

Is such radical institutional revision easy or even possible? Perhaps not, or perhaps not without risk or struggle. Underpinning the work of this chapter and the entire book, however, is a commitment to critical visions of hope as an important tool for articulating possible futures that move beyond institutional critique. We need to envision ethical and productive partnerships in order to create them. I therefore end the chapter with a meditation on hope as an important, imaginative function that can and does inform the important work we do, in the streets and in the classroom.

Debating the Public Roles of Teachers, Writers, and Scholars

Recently, within a wide range of popular and academic venues, questions and anxieties about the public responsibilities—or some may say duties—of academics have begun to circulate. Calls for the working lives of academics to be relevant and engaged with pressing matters are often countered by criticisms alleging that the push for local engagement comes as the result of an identity crisis in education and thus "thrusts faculty members into roles for which they are ill equipped" (Nelson 2002, 713). Writers debate where academics should draw the boundaries of territory they can claim either as local experts or as participants within civic debates. Arguing for a limited boundary of scholarship, Stanley Fish (2004) claims that academics should only concern themselves with matters within "the Ivory Tower," and not feel an obligation to "save the world" (23).[1] Other writers, like Cary Nelson (2002), hold out hope for the emergence of "citizen scholars" but worry that academics have "efficient mechanisms for deluding themselves" with regard to how well equipped they are for assuming this role. Despite his anxiety, Nelson advocates drawing broad and permeable borders for academic work, encouraging scholars to "identify not only with institution and discipline but also with community," especially in terms of labor struggles (713).

Michael Bérubé (1998) encourage academics to find points of connection between their scholarship and current national policy debates. He explores both the possibilities and risk involved in "selling out" one's work to popular reading audiences: "[O]ur task in selling out is not to capitulate to the terms our historical moment has offered us, but rather to find the terms with which we can best *contest* those terms, and in so doing redescribe and redefine both our cultural politics and our social policies" (249). In this way, Bérubé defines the public role of cultural-studies academics as rhetoricians, with a responsibility to frame, question, and directly engage in policy debates, at least in a written form.

The field of rhetoric and composition intersects repeatedly with questions about public work in its scholarship and teaching. Edward Schiappa (1995) argues that scholars and teachers of rhetoric have not only a right but a responsibility to engage in local political debates—an argument with ancient roots in the work of Sophistic philosophers who theorized and taught rhetorical practice while directly engaging contemporary political issues. For Schiappa, teaching and researching rhetoric is not enough if one wants to remain credible in the eyes of our students. "We take pride in the values and critical tools with which we equip our students, but if they do not *also* see us in the trenches, so to speak, then they know our values and critical tools are *merely* academic" (22). In order to avoid what he calls "trickle down citizenship participation" (teaching rhetorical skills without employing them directly), Schiappa recommends that faculty hone their rhetorical knowledge by regularly participating in politics, writing for local campaigns and newspaper columns. Similarly, Peter Mortenson (1998) argues that writing scholars should directly inform public and political debates about literacy and education, drawing from scholarship and teaching knowledge gained within composition classrooms. His vision advocates foregrounding a concern for ethics in such work by anchoring it "in national concerns, but it must attend to the local because it is there that political and social issues of great consequence can be deliberated and acted upon" (198). Both Schiappa and Mortensen advocate a more porous boundary demarcating inside and outside the academy to allow knowledge and expertise to flow in both directions between campus and street. Their vision encourages academics to add a public-writing component to their traditional research or scholarship in rhetoric and literacy.

For others in composition, public work leads more directly to scholarship and research projects. The history of composition scholarship boasts much work grounded in what Gere (1994) calls the "extracurriculum of composition"—studying literacy practices of local communities outside academic communities for important lessons about the way people use and interact with writing.[2] Ellen Cushman (1999, 2002b) endorses the public value of conducting research in local communities, arguing that academic research should ground long-term faculty commitments in local communities. Katrina Powell and Pamela Takayoshi (2002) argue that community research projects must be grounded in a ongoing notion of reciprocity, which is seen as an original process between researcher and participants.

Frank Farmer (2002) advocates a self-critical vision of "community intellectuals," which foregrounds the needs and purposes that define the *public* at a given moment. "What community intellectuals do," he writes, "is *embody* intellectual work, give it a human face, a face able to confront the human faces of our neighbors and citizens in a cooperative spirit of making communities better—more hopeful, more sustainable, more just places to live" (210). Farmer's vision includes teaching, scholarship, and service, as does Chris Gallagher's conception of "pedagogy-centered outreach" (2002, 177–185). Gallagher argues that public work of scholars in composition has too often neglected connections to public schools and advocates a conception of outreach "that would encourage and highlight cross-institutional alliances" (185).

Some arguments for academics working within local communities are grounded in administrative endeavors to construct university-community alliances. Eli Goldblatt and Stephen Parks (2002) argue that writing across the curriculum lends itself to looking beyond academic disciplines to "the writing demands in various local constituencies" (600). They describe the Temple University Institute for the Study of Literature, Literacy, and Culture as "an alliance of university, public school and community educators" which aims to define the university writing program in terms that stretch beyond curricular and campus boundaries. Similarly, the Carnegie Mellon Community Literacy

Center seeks to formalize partnerships with university researchers, students, and various community groups (Flower 2000; 2002).

While writers who take on questions of public and civic responsibility generally support including such work as part of the profile of a teacher/writer/scholar, many also offer warnings about the dangers and limits of such endeavors. While advocating public writing, Bérubé (1998) admits the limited effect it can have on political life: "Despite my efforts to historicize, decontruct, and redefine the arguments of my opponents, I actually have not had all that much impact on national policy myself" (233). Farmer (2002) raises fundamental questions of how and on whose behalf academics construct their understanding of public needs: [How do we] define—perhaps more accurately redefine—the public intellectual to meet *our* needs and purposes in *our* moment? (And more problematic I think: Who exactly constitutes membership in the pronouns of my question?)" (21). Gallagher (2002) worries that academic outreach has been defined by a "'public service' ethos that easily lends itself to condescension, paternalism and missionary zeal" (185). Clyde Moneyhun (2000) "wonder[s] if research is an inherently parasitic activity, and the most you can do is mitigate that parasitism as much as possible." In describing a community-literacy research project he had undertaken, Moneyhun explores the hurt feelings and difficult political choices that punctuated the process, which was ironically tempered by the "the reassurance of the program director that in the big picture, my research could do little harm, as nobody would read it anyway."

Arguing for visions of pedagogy and scholarship that attend more closely to the sites in which such interactions occur, Di Leo, Jacobs, and Lee (2002) give the following warning:

> [E]ven those of us with the best intentions can reproduce conditions of injustice, silencing, objectification and prejudice within our classrooms or our research. Regardless of how much we aim to represent the historically Othered, those excluded from and marginalized within academia, we must be careful not to speak for them. Rather, we must learn from and with them about the limits and possibilities of what we have imagined and envisioned. (11)

While critical concerns circulate within academic writing about the public work of academics, such criticisms rarely question the disciplinary or institutional paradigms that define accepted practices for scholarship and teaching. The desire to engage the civic responsibility of the teacher/writer/scholar can be undermined or turned into an exploitive situation when such desires are spurred or reshaped by the institutional paradigms that define the work life of an academic in terms of research, teaching, and service. I do not advocate ducking institutional responsibilities; I believe that the relatively privileged life of many university workers does and should entail the cost of accountability. Rather, I'm concerned that disciplinary conceptions of what rhetorical research, teaching, and service look like have been limited by what Joseph Harris calls, "composition's struggle to build credibility within the academy," a struggle that he asserts "has been a full time job" (182).

The pressures to institutionalize and professionalize English studies have directly inhibited intellectual renovations that seek to move beyond disciplinary modes of working, argues David Downing in "Beyond Disciplinary English" (2002). Downing traces the making of English studies "into a respectable academic discipline" as a process that has required defining a specific body of knowledge, specific methods with which to explore that knowledge, and an agreement that all methods depend on protocols largely derived from logic and the sciences (24). While disciplining has helped establish the strategic value for English studies within universities, Downing argues that such development comes at a cost: "While the strict processes of disciplining have become the quintessential measure of academic value, the institutionalized protocols for disciplinary practices often exclude or delimit a significant range of socially valuable intellectual labor" (26). The disciplinary development of English places severe limits on academics' ability to draw the boundaries of their loyalties to include entities outside the university and routinely causes community members affected by local projects to be excluded from means of assessment:

> The disciplinary measure of success, therefore, purposefully displaces any accountability to people immediately affected by a practical innovation, such as the development of an interactive website linking local high school, community college and university English departments in a collaborative network. Although it is no doubt possible to give credit for such work, disciplinary pressure will inevitably tend to give greater significance to the published article about the website than reward those who created it and participated in its ongoing success. (Downing 2000, 26)

Sharon O'Dair (2004) echoes a similar sentiment, arguing that in academia, status accrues to those whose work remains abstract and distanced from everyday life: "The more abstract the problems one deals with, the more status one achieves in one's field; the more one deals with messy human beings, and in particular with messy low-status human beings, the less status one achieves in one's field" (564). Therefore, in order to achieve status while working in local communities, some academics turn to research or teaching projects that serve to enhance their academic profile but may not serve the community in whose names they work. While seeking public engagement, pressures for publishing and displaying a professional body of work can lead to exploitive or unproductive relationships. The following example shows what can happen when academics try to simultaneously "do good work" and reap institutional praise.

An Academic Horror Story

When institutional priorities intersect with community needs, people can get hurt. Projects can lead to bitterness and disillusionment. The following true story shows what can happen when desires for academic achievement eclipse one's ability to be responsive to community needs. I have erased specific references and changed names to protect both the innocent and the not-so-innocent.

Jane was a formerly homeless veteran and an outreach worker for a community group of homeless and socially excluded people, which worked under the umbrella of a large nonprofit. The group's members decided to collect stories and writing by local homeless people and compile it into an anthology of writing. They hoped to get help from local universities and the sponsoring nonprofit in order to, as Jane said, "educate the general public about homelessness" ("Jane" 2004). Eventually, this collaboration involved two local universities that offered to involve students in service-learning projects to help with collecting stories and preparing the manuscript. The proceeds from the project were to create a small community fund to which low-income individuals could apply, to pay for small but important life or work items, such as state IDs or steel-toed boots for work on a construction site. The fund would be managed by a panel of homeless and formerly homeless people who would hear cases and decide if the needs were real and couldn't be met elsewhere in the community. "If it were real," Jane said, "we would lend the applicant funds from the book profits, and they would pay back when they were better situated or they could join the project and pay back in other ways."

While leery about partnering with bigger institutions, Jane said the unsheltered participants saw the promise of a connection that would "pull together people from a variety of socioeconomic backgrounds. Our idea was that students would hear stories and help with the work of the book, but they would also make human connections and become more knowledgeable about the reasons people become homeless." The offers of help seemed genuine, she said: "One college also offered to help us publish the book, not edit, not control."

The group warmed to the idea and decided to pursue it, but it didn't turn out as planned. "Too many people were involved," Jane said, "and with too many agendas. [One of the colleges involved in the service project] and [the nonprofit governing our group] had shared board members. This was a threatening structure, because both the college and the nonprofit had big plans for themselves as being seen as good people in the neighborhood." Eventually, the second participating college dropped out of the project.

While the goal of the service learning was to involve students in collecting stories, during the spring semester "no students had shown up to come to the street and talk to people . . . [Also] the college had appointed an intern who was to be a liaison to the project, but I never even met her; she was just a name on the paper," Jane said.

The English professor involved in the service-learning project asked Jane for poems and stories to be used for readings in his classes, so four members of the community group collected stories and wrote some of their own.

> I wrote a bunch of examples. They were not intended to be part of the book—they were just stories for use in the class. I even drew a black ink X across claiming them as examples . . . of what might come in, with time and the help of the students that the college had promised. I had hoped we would do more the next semester. ("Jane" 2004)

Jane's group, while focusing on pressing legislative issues affecting homeless people, continued working on the project after the spring semester had ended. "During the summer, our group continued work, even talking with a formerly homeless man who operates a printing business. We were busy collecting stories, people would even mail them in from the jail or other such places."

The service-learning professor was having a very busy summer as well. Jane recalls an article that ran in the college's student newspaper, naming the service-learning professor as editor of the book project. "I called the reporter asking for a correction," she said. Even though the paper acknowledged a mistake, the information sadly proved correct.

The English professor published a book that summer, using the community group's name as the title of the book, without their permission, and claiming himself as editor of the project, despite the fact he had never gathered a single story. "He took control of the book publishing without ever talking to us, only getting the okay from our sponsoring nonprofit (shared board members, remember)." Jane and her colleagues who worked with the homeless writers gathering the stories and compiling the manuscript received no credit whatsoever. Even worse, the contents of the printed manuscript were a mix of real stories and examples, according to Jane:

> He used all the stories, including the examples I had written for his service-learning students, as if actual people had written them. Even though the book claims to be poems and stories by homeless writers,

the professor even published one of his own poems," she said. "And [by] the way, the book [was] copyrighted. The 26 writers whose work I had collected lost rights to their work . . . . The book appeared everywhere and the professor claims credit for collecting and editing the stories and for the book design, which all came from our group. (2004)

The profits from the book did not go into a community fund but rather into the operating costs of the governing nonprofit. Jane claims that the overall project "has been empowering for some, while it has been oppressive for others." One of the project organizers now "is incarcerated. He felt so powerless through all of this that he gave up his dreams and went back to the bottle from which he dragged himself . . . the book states he went onto college, but he never got past the admissions office." Six of the writers died while the book was in production, and three more have died since then, according to Jane. "I don't know what else to tell you," she added.

As for herself, Jane says this project left her feeling much pain and resentment. Surprisingly, however, she has not given up altogether on the hope of working with students and universities in the future: "I have let go of the resentments. I have had to in order to survive and move on . . . I still believe in the process. I believe that local colleges and universities play an important role in supporting local initiatives even though it has been complicated."

I asked Jane what suggestions she would give to faculty who are or will be involved with community partnerships; she offered the following list, which I share in its entirety:

1. Let the people decide!
2. Your job as a college group is not to lead but to allow the [community] group to gain some power as you facilitate access to resources.
3. Don't set the timeline according to when your semester ends or when you need grades. Try to allow the project to grow on its own course, even if your class is finished.
4. For students requiring grades for work: Submit progress notes and ongoing project aspirations. It is about progress, not the product.
5. If you set yourself up as leader, then you must always be there to lead. If you inspire others to act on their own behalf, they will continue to do so when you no longer need them.
6. Don't take the glory for the work but raise up members of the group to feel honored for the work. It goes a long way for self-esteem and group esteem.

7. You don't have the authority to make decisions for others; you have not been where they have. You don't need the power now; you will get it in other ways throughout your life. This may be their only chance to feel like a winner.

8. Whatever the issue, don't assume that you know the answers because you have talked to a few people. Once you think you have found an answer, research some more via conversations about the issue with people in the group. Don't be surprised if they don't give you textbook answers.

9. Remember that this isn't about the grade or tenure; it is about changing lives.

10. Continue to look for opportunities to serve. Be willing to be radical, theatrical and otherwise suggest ideas that haven't been tried before.

It is easy to vilify the unnamed professor in this story. It is tempting to individualize this situation and find this person and his or her actions unethical and disgraceful—a cartoonish horror story not unlike the fictional academics I discuss in the Introduction. Even more chilling, however, is to understand how easily hurtful situations like this can occur: Good intentions and enthusiasm, coupled with limited communication with community partners, driven by desires for markers of disciplinary success, are a recipe for disaster. Academics want investments of time and efforts to bear fruit, and without extreme caution and the ability to adapt, wait, or put on the brakes, that desire can lead to partnerships that, as Jane described, are "empowering to some and oppressive to others."

From Horrors to Heroes

If the standard disciplinary markers for academic success and organization—publication guidelines, semester schedules, tenure clocks, grading criteria, etc.—can make conditions ripe for exploiting local groups, can we find alternate ways for defining academic success? David Downing (2002) argues that now may be an apt time to question and move beyond traditional disciplinary measures of academic performance:

> There are possibilities for retooling evaluation practices and re*vision-ing* humanities' labor as running across a spectrum of disciplinary and extra-, non-, or postdisciplinary activities that need not be measured according to a single yardstick. And the human labor involved in these practices calls for revaluations throughout our professional ranks as we re*imagine* the activities of reading and writing our cultures for a better future. (35)

It is beyond the scope of this book for me to outline what such reimagined measures or guidelines for the academic performance of a streetwise academic would look like. Instead, I offer a first step by considering useful examples of people doing good work, despite institutional constraints. These individuals—a graduate student, a full professor, and an internationally known academic and activist—are just three of the many people doing amazing work everyday in local communities, who don't allow their work to be defined or confined by the strategic demands of institutions and professionalization. From Sandra Andrews, Diana George, Howard Zinn, and many others, we can learn much about working in the streets and can find sources of inspiration and hope.

Sandra Andrews

In Chapter 3, I described Tom Boland and his work with the Homeless People's Network (HPN), an archived email listserv open to people who have experienced homelessness. The list came about in 1997 because of the efforts of one graduate student in educational media and technology at Arizona State University, Sandra Andrews. Throughout her graduate work, Sandra developed questions as to how technology could realize its potential to link together all people, especially "those who had fallen through the cracks" (Andrews 2004). She didn't have clear answers, just this interest and a desire to learn more.

To educate herself, Sandra signed on to an early listserv about homeless issues. Over time, Sandra noticed that the voices of "people who had been homeless were being drowned out by service providers," which led to some complaints and friction on the list. She said she was considering forming a separate list when Tom Boland posted a message echoing the same concern. Tom remembers it this way:

> Sandra's first contact with me was very personal and was unrelated to her career. She had been on an international homeless discussion list and I made a call to form a listserv just for homeless people. She responded as a human being, a caring person, who was interested in my work. That year, she sent me $89 to take a bus to Arizona so we could meet. She had another project with Arizona State University and knew they were doing technology projects in the community. We talked about whether HPN might fit that mission. (Boland 2004)

Sandra says that underlying this partnership was the belief that neither she nor the university had the final answers or solutions, and that the partnership would truly have to be defined by the community group:

> Tom insisted that the listserv would be open only to people who had experienced homelessness, that the university wouldn't control its

content, and that it could be removed from the university at any time. The general public could read any of the material on an archives Web page. The university would just provide the Web page, support, firewalls, and security. We set the project up just the way Tom wanted it, with two goals. One, to allow people to have a voice. Two, to build archives of solutions. The archives will provide a place for people interested in finding solutions to homelessness that are vetted by people who have been in the situation. (Andrews 2004)

While Sandra has not performed what might be defined as traditional academic research in terms of this project, she highlights the public and academic value of making a public archive of the HPN discussions: "There's no say on the part of the university as to how HPN gets used. The archives are in the public domain, open to researchers and policy makers. We want people to investigate this as data and use the ideas to generate solutions." Her work demonstrates that one needn't wait to attain faculty status to develop partnerships with local groups that tie into university resources and expertise. More importantly, her method of working with the HPN shows that important social and rhetorical outcomes for university-community partnerships need not—and often should not—take on traditional academic forms.

Diana George

Diana George, a professor of English specializing in composition and rhetoric at Michigan Technological University, spent a sabbatical year living and working at the Open Door in Atlanta, an intentional community that seeks to live in community with and serve those who are homeless, poor, or in prison. At this place that some call a "Protestant Catholic Worker House," Diana worked daily to prepare breakfast for the homeless community, distribute clothes and toiletries to people in need, and help publish the community's monthly alternative newspaper, *Hospitality*. Her husband, Chuck, started volunteering at the Open Door six years ago, when Diana was a visiting professor at Clemson University. After spending some vacation time there over the next five winters, the two agreed to spend an extended time at the Open Door.

Diana's life at the Open Door looked quite different than a typical academic schedule. The morning reflection meeting began at 5:45 A.M., where she met with the 15 to 20 other residents to discuss the work of the house in "an action-reflection" format until about 6:30 A.M. "Before that," she said, "someone's been up since 4 A.M. making grits and eggs. Someone else is up at 3:00 making coffee. We start serving breakfast by 7:00. I'm usually in the sorting room, giving out clothes, soap, etc., until about 9:30. We don't eat until everyone else has" (George 2004). The rest of her days were filled with meetings to coordinate the needs of the community, bread and milk runs, lunch, house duty, and editorial work on *Hospitality*, which includes writing, editing, and responding to readers' correspondence. It's been adjusting to this scheduled life, Diana admitted, that has been the most difficult: "I have been amazingly privileged. I'm used to spending my time as I choose. Now I can't have my own car, have to sign out on the board. That's so strange to me, but I realize many people live their lives on tight schedules."

While her time there was considered a sabbatical, Diana didn't go to the Open Door with a specific research project in mind, and this was an explicit decision:

> I was hesitant to use this experience for me. There are things that need to be written about, and I hope I will write about some of those things for larger audiences someday. But the ethics of being in a place not to do the work but to get something out of it for your career has been a defining concern for me . . . . I like writing [in *Hospitality*] about the issues I encounter here but am still concerned about using people and the experience for my career. (2004)

While no overarching *strategic* plan guided her work at the Open Door, Diana admitted that she has learned many things that will affect her research and teaching in the future:

> Even though I knew it politically, I hadn't experienced the lack of understanding that governments have for the real needs out there. The things I have written about and critiqued as an academic—the ridiculous division between deserving and undeserving poor, for example—I knew but didn't really understand until I had to face it every day. I now understand that our healthcare system is completely inadequate. I see people everyday with their teeth falling out or who are sick on the streets and can't get the attention they need. The level of need out there, given the number of people with HIV and other kinds of illnesses, is staggering. The inability to get dental care or any pair of glasses is a testimony to the failures of this country . . . . The realities of the inadequate care we give to "the least" in our country are astounding. I say it that way because we are a nation that claims itself as Christian—a bad claim anyway. But if we do claim that, "Whatever you do for the least, you do for Me" is a centerpiece of Christian gospel, it is not the way that most Christians or the government in this country function.

When asked about how her work has informed her experiences as a teacher and a writer, Diana focused on her work at *Hospitality*, which has changed how she writes and has caused her to think more deeply about public writing and the teaching of public writing:[3]

This writing frees me up to be a bit outrageous—I write columns and opinion pieces and speak directly to media concerns. I write on deadline. I write something in nearly every monthly issue. This connects to my teaching because I want my students to learn something that matters. To do that students have to read and write something that matters, which can make a difference in how politics are conceived or conveyed—things that move you in different ways, not just on a personal level. Part of what I think the writing classroom has to do is not to rest within literary genres, even though there's beauty there, and seek to understand public discourse . . . . [Working here] I have learned there's a lot of information and dialogue taking place in small publications, on flyers, on posters that's crucial for students and faculty to be part of.

Finally, Diana articulates that, while care needs to be taken, there are important research questions and projects for academics to pursue in the community:

We need to know what's going on, because the government claims to know what is going on, with homelessness, healthcare, education. Most of what they claim is falsified or skewed . . . we need to come back with knowledge, not just anger. When Anne Gere goes to a group of women and wants to know what's going on there, how will this help me figure out what's going on in the classroom? That's an important kind of question. But when someone goes into the community and decides they want to be a good person who assigns their students service work, that's a bad project. It comes down to questioning so our work in the community will not become a career-building move.

Diana George offers an example of an academic working in a low-income community without a direct line to a research project or academic publication. Her interests are grounded in and shaped by interests in public discourse and the efficacy of public rhetoric to bring about societal change. Her writing and service work will continue to inform and shape her future teaching, research, and service, but the connection she made at the Open Door was not a transactional means to further specific work. Writing or research may follow or grow from this kind of experience, but should not be a starting point for local connections.

Howard Zinn

If anyone can answer Diana George's question—How do we create community projects that aren't merely exercises in careerism?— it would be noted historian and activist Howard Zinn. Howard is world-renowned as a leftist writer who highlights marginalized versions of history and an outspoken activist who takes public stands against acts of war. Howard has become something of a national hero, celebrated in film and art.[4] He is someone who has reached a wide readership through his books and articles in news magazines such as *Harper's, The Nation,* and *The Progressive.* His *People's History of the United States* has sold more than one million copies, and sales continue to increase twenty-five years after its original release. His memoir is also a best-seller, and a documentary of his life has been touring the country. Even though he enjoys international notoriety, Howard remains quietly connected to local issues in the Boston metropolitan area, making himself available to speak at local events and to small organizations—like the local street paper, *Spare Change News*—even though he's past 80 years old. In 2002, when the North American Street Newspaper Association held its convention in Boston, Howard agreed to be the keynote speaker, charged nothing for his talk, and spent much of an afternoon having lunch, speaking, and answering questions of our group. When asked about how he balances notoriety with local connectedness, he gave the following reply:

> Sure it's easy to get an inflated view of your own importance when other people say extravagant things. It helps to live with someone who brings you down to earth from time to time. I used to think I couldn't say no to someone who wanted me to speak somewhere or show up somewhere, thinking, I suppose subconsciously, that I was indispensable. But at a certain point I realized this was not true. (2004)

It might be easy to look at Howard's current iconic status and assume that it's easy to be gracious and involved in one's community after achieving international acclaim. But what's remarkable about Howard Zinn is that his career has been intertwined with political struggles since before his first academic job as an assistant professor at Spelman College in 1959. He was willing to incur risks in the name of work that was important to him and willing to face the consequences of his actions. As an assistant professor at a black college, he became involved in desegregation struggles in the southern United States—not as a leader but taking the lead of his students—and began writing about the growing movement in publications like *The Nation*:

> My writing came out of my activism in the [desegregation] movement and my desire to tell people what was happening in the South. I didn't think in terms of building up my cv . . . but in terms of what kind of writing can be helpful to the movement at the time. My first article was in *Harper's* in 1959 about the thinking of whites in the south. I wrote it because I thought it would be tactically helpful to write about what was behind racism, how racist behavior could be overcome.

Being involved, however, meant being in the line of fire, especially when the debates involved campus issues. In 1963, Howard supported a student initiative to liberalize campus rules and curricula at Spelman. At the end of that school year, despite his tenure, he received a letter letting him know that his contract would not be renewed.[5] Ultimately, supporting student initiatives for local change cost him his job. Rather than engage in a legal battle, he moved on to Boston University, where he continued to be involved with institutional and political issues for several decades, especially protests against the Vietnam War. On the very day that his tenure case was being decided by the university's trustees, Howard accepted a student invitation to be the sole faculty member to speak at an antiwar rally in front of the very building where the trustees were meeting to decide his tenure case. While he received tenure, his legendary battles with Boston University President John Silber regularly left Howard with high teaching loads and no graduate assistants.[6] When asked what advice he would give to young academics wanting to engage local matters, he foregrounded the need to understand risks and limits:

> If you want to be a social activist in the academic world, you're risking tenure, getting fired. It's not inevitable, but it's a risk you have to have to accept . . . . Every person has a different level of risk and social conscience . . . Every person has to decide how far they're willing to go.

Howard's rich and ongoing legacy of courage, commitment, and most importantly, humility offers a model of academic life that takes part in history and takes risks in order to "bring to light those stories which would motivate people to act about injustice" (Zinn 2004).

Learning from Our Heroes

Sandra Andrews, Diana George, and Howard Zinn—and countless other teachers working in high schools, colleges, and universities today—exemplify what I consider to be tactical and hopeful academic work. Their connections with various communities arise organically, often through personal connections and investment of time rather than professional decisions or agendas. Their work is largely project-based, with needs and parameters of projects defined by the constituencies involved. The output or products of the work don't fit disciplinary definitions of academic research and take on unconventional forms, such as community archives and general-interest articles. The projects are all rhetorical, guided by tactical concerns for timeliness and relevance, which define their form. What these projects all share is a belief in the value of local knowledge to intervene in and affect national and international debates and frame the role of the academic as facilitator in the circulation of marginalized points of view. The benefits of such work may or may not be recognized within institutional frameworks, and the risks of engaging such work can be significant. Certainty rarely guides tactical projects. A tactical academic balances personal convictions with close connections and dialogue about the work he or she does, not to arrive at final answers but to build some useful projects that hopefully will do good work in the world.

A Meditation on Hope

Many eloquent words have been written about hope by Ernst Bloch and others (see Chapter 1). Bloch's philosophical work on hope reminds us that hoping is not a naïve or wishful act, but is a critical, active process of "militant optimism" (1986, 146), which requires an ever reflective utopian process of acknowledging the radical insufficiency of the present and envisioning the future. Hope does not offer a blueprint to follow, but compels a critical function of engagement.

Other writers and teachers have written about hope as an essential function of life and work. I can think of no better way to end this book than to offer a meditation on hope, including the words from several key teachers, writers, and activists who can teach us much about hope. To Paulo Freire (1997), hope is a restlessness of mind and spirit that drives the pursuit of justice:

> Hope is rooted in men's [sic] incompletion, from which they move out in constant search—a search which can be carried out only in communion with others. Hopelessness is a form of silence, of denying the world and fleeing from it. The dehumanization resulting from an unjust order is not a cause for despair but for hope, leading to the incessant pursuit of the humanity denied by injustice. Hope, however, does not consist in crossing one's arms and waiting. As long as I fight, I am moved by hope; and if I fight with hope, then I can wait. (72–73)

To oral historian and radio commentator Studs Terkel (2003), hope is essentially a bottom-up activity that is essential to combating despair and cynicism:

> It's easy to talk yourself into despair. Hope is physical and visceral. I don't think you can talk yourself into it. I think you have to *do* yourself into it. The more people try things, work at things, test things, push boundaries, experiment, the less we just angst about it, the better. (242)

To Howard Zinn, hope is an "insistence," an active decision he made after he returned home from World War II when many of his comrades did not, a declaration that he "has no right to despair" (1994, 12). Hopefulness, to Zinn, requires understanding history, learning how change happens in the world through the efforts of many people:

> We don't have to engage in grand, heroic actions to participate in a process of change. Small acts, when multiplied by millions of people, can transform the world.
>
> To be hopeful in bad times is not just foolishly romantic. It is based on the fact that human history is a history not only of cruelty, but also of compassion, sacrifice, courage, kindness.
>
> What we choose to emphasize in this complex history will determine our lives. If we see only the worst, it destroys our capacity to do something. If we remember those times and places—and there are so many—where people have behaved magnificently, this gives us energy to act, and at least the possibility of sending this spinning top of a world in a different direction.
>
> And if we do act, in however a small way, we don't have to wait for some grand utopian future. The future is an infinite succession of presents, and to live *now* as we think human beings should live, in defiance of all that is bad around us, is itself a marvelous victory. (1994, 208)

To Diana George, hope is a small but insistent need to keep working, not for certain outcomes, but because it's the just and necessary thing to do:

> You can't hope to change the system, because at some point you'll get so disappointed you'll quit. You can't hope that you'll be the instrument of change at any point. I give someone a T-shirt in the morning. Maybe now they have a shirt, but maybe not. Maybe they sold the shirt or maybe someone took it from them. If you're working on the streets, despite the fact that your friends think you're doing a lot, you realize how little you're doing, how huge the problems are. When people you care about congratulate you about your work, all you can think is, "I don't do much."
>
> I think the hope is a small thing. The old political slogan "Think globally/act locally" is still important to me. I cannot hope to change Atlanta city government, but I refuse to stop trying because it might happen. Things do happen incrementally. People like Dorothy Day and Peter Maurin were in and out of jail all the time, for example. Even a small thing like air-raid warnings in NYC that [Day] refused to go inside for—after a while her little group would get arrested. But eventually there were hundreds of New Yorkers doing that—there was a movement. There are moments where small things change, but you can't count on that. All you can hope for is a life lived intentionally where

you can't rest with injustice, where you keep saying it shouldn't be that
way, or the Mayor is a liar . . . you have to keep saying it. (2004)

These statements—and the stories I share throughout this book—
attest to a critical practice that moves beyond critique toward always-
tentative, always-insufficient tactical responses. Hope, defined in
critical terms, requires the ability to recognize the radical insufficiency
of any actions, be honest in assessing their limitations, imagine better
ways to act and learn, and despite the real limitations, engage creative
acts of work and play with an eye toward a better not-yet future.

I have deep concerns about university partnerships with the
streets, but I insist on hope for going forward, the kind of hope that
doesn't offer a predetermined blueprint for future practices but
demands a critical interrogation of the present to accompany any
action that results. This book is just one partial gesture, grounded in
hope, that imagines street partnerships as project-based and tactical.
Tactical projects are limited by, yet given life and specificity by, spatial
and temporal demands and a self-reflexive rhetorical nature; they
aren't likely to be easily replicable or generalizable; they may be
unpopular or risky. But they are likely to be useful to local communities and may even help academics imagine new post-disciplinary forms
of research. Working tactically in a university setting may be unpredictable and inefficient, but it is an act of hope.

Notes

1. E.g., Fish; Weisser (on Fish); and O'Dair.
2. E.g., Street; Heath; Goldblatt and Parks; Nardini.
3. See George 2002, 2004.
4. See Zinn 1994, 2004. For a painted tribute, see http://www.americans-
    whotellthetruth.org.
5. See Zinn 1994, Chapter 3.
6. See Zinn 2004.

Works Cited

Abel, David. 16 September 2002. "To Her, It's Home." *Boston Globe*: B4+.

Adler-Kassner, Linda, Robert Crooks, and Ann Watters, eds. 1997. *Writing the Community: Concepts and Models for Service-Learning in Composition*. Washington, D.C.: American Association for Higher Education Press.

Anderson, Virginia. 1997. "Confrontational Teaching and Rhetorical Practice." *College Composition and Communication* 48(2): 197–214.

Andrews, Sandra. 24 June 2004. Telephone interview.

Aronowitz, Stanley. (2000). *The Knowledge Factory: Dismantling the Corporate University and Creating True Higher Learning*. Boston, MA: Beacon Press.

Bacon, Nora. 1997. "Community Service Writing: Problems, Challenges, Questions." In *Writing the Community: Concepts and Models for Service-Learning in Composition*. Linda Adler-Kassner, Robert Crooks, and Ann Watters, eds. Washington, D.C.: American Association for Higher Education Press. 39–56.

Baker Jr., Houston A. 1993. "Local Pedagogy: Or, How I Redeemed My Spring Semester." *Publications of the Modern Language Association*. 108(3): 400–409.

Bard, Marjorie. 1990. *Shadow Women: Homeless Women's Survival Stories*. Lanham, MD: Rowman & Littlefield.

Bennett, B. Cole. 2000. "The Best of Intentions: Service-Learning and Noblesse Oblige at a Christian College." *Reflections*. 1(2): 18–23.

Berlin, James A. 1996. *Rhetorics, Poetics, and Cultures*. Urbana, IL: National Council of Teachers of English.

———. 1990. "Writing Instruction in School and College English, 1890–1985." In *A Short History of Writing Instruction: From Ancient Greece to 20th Century America*. Ed. James Murphy. Davis, CA: Hermagoras Press. 182–220.

Berlin, James, and Michael Vivion, eds. 1992. *Cultural Studies in the English Classroom*. Portsmouth, NH: Boynton, Cook/Heinneman.

Bérubé, Michael. 1998. *The Employment of English*. New York: New York University Press.

Blau, Joel. 1992. *The Visible Poor: Homelessness in the United States*. New York: Oxford University Press.

Blitz, Michael, and C. Mark Hurlbert. 1998. *Letters for the Living: Teaching Writing in a Violent Age*. Urbana, IL: National Council of Teachers of English.

Blitz, Michael, Dan Collins, Nancy Dunlop, Ellen Grimes, C. Mark Hurlbert, Annie Knepler, Paula Mathieu, and Derek Owens. 1999–2000."Between (E)utopia and Apocalypse: Narrative In and Out of Cyberspace." *Works and Days*. 33-36: Eds. Gian Pagnucci and Nick Mauriello. 453–487.

Bloch, Ernst. 1986. *Principle of Hope*. Vol. 1. Translated by Neville Plaice, Stephen Plaice, and Paul Knight. Cambridge, MA: MIT Press.

———. 1998. *The Utopian Function of Art and Literature: Selected Essays*. Cambridge, MA: MIT Press.

Boland, Tom. 15 January 2004. Personal interview.

Brack, Gay W., and Leanna Hall. 1997. "Combining the Classroom and the Community: Service-Learning in Composition at Arizona State University." In *Writing the Community: Concepts and Models for Service-Learning in Composition*. Linda Adler-Kassner, Robert Crooks, and Ann Watters, eds. Washington, D.C.: American Association for Higher Education Press. 143–152.

Brandt, Deborah. 2001. *Literacy in American Lives*. New York: Cambridge University Press.

Bridwell-Bowles, Lillian. 1997. "Service Learning: Help for Higher Education in a New Milennium?" In *Writing the Community: Concepts and Models for Service-Learning in Composition*. Linda Adler-Kassner, Robert Crooks, and Ann Watters, eds. Washington, D.C.: American Association for Higher Education Press. 1998. 19–28.

Buccola, Gina. 2000. "Not Your Mama's Bus Tour: This Bus'll School Ya." Online Review. Big Shoulders Website. http://www.sobs.org.

"C." 24 May 2003. Personal interview.

Candyman. 1992. Directed by Bernard Rose. PolyGram.

Campus Compact. 2004a. "About Campus Compact: What We've Done: An 18-Year Retrospective." http://www.compact.org/aboutcc/retrospective/retrospective.html.

———. 2004b. "Benchmarks for Campus/Community Partnerships." http://www.compact.org/ccpartnerships/benchmarks-overview.html.

Campus Compact. "Wingspread Declaration on the Civic Responsibilities of Research Universities." 1999. http://www.compact.org/civic/Wingspread/Wingspread.html. 14 April 2004.

Carrick, Tracy Hamler, Margaret Himley, and Tobi Jacobi. 2000. "Ruptura: Acknowledging the Lost Subjects of the Service Learning Story." *Language and Learning Across the Disciplines* 4:3: 56–75.

Cassell, Susie Lan. (2000). "Hunger for Memory: Oral History Recovery in Community Service Learning." *Reflections* 1:2. 12–17.

The Caveman's Valentine. 2001. Directed by Kasi Lemmons. Arroyo Pictures.

de Certeau, Michel. 1984. *The Practice of Everyday Life*. Translated by Steven Rendall. Berkeley, CA: University of California Press. 1988.

Chaden, Caryn, Roger Graves, David A. Jolliffe, and Peter Vandenberg. 2002. "Confronting Clashing Discourses: Writing the Space Between Classroom and Community in Service-Learning Courses." *Reflections* 2(2): 19–39.

Clark, Gregory. 1998. "Writing as Travel, or Rhetoric on the Road." *College Composition and Communication.* 49(1): 9–23.

Collins, Daniel. 2001. "The Great Work: Recomposing Vocationalism and the Community College English Curriculum." In *Beyond English, Inc: Curricular Reform in a Global Economy.* David Downing, Claude Mark Hurlbert, and Paula Mathieu, eds. Portsmouth, NH: Boynton/Cook Heinemann. 2002. 194–203.

Conference on College Composition and Communication. 2001. "CCC 2002 Annual Convention." http://www.ncte.org/convention/cccc2002/theme.shtml.

Conference on College Composition and Communication. "Call for Papers: CCCC 2002." http://www.ncte.org/profdev/conv/cccc. 12 December 2001.

Conversations on Jesuit Higher Education. 2003. 23, Spring.

Cooper, David D., and Laura Julier. 1995. "Democratic Conversations: Civic Literacy and Service-Learning in the American Grains." In *Writing the Community: Concepts and Models for Service-Learning in Composotion.* Linda Adler-Kassner, Robert Crooks, and Ann Watters, eds. Washington, D.C.: American Association for Higher Education Press. 1997. 79–94.

Cooper, Marilyn. 2003. "From the Editor." *College Composition and Communication.* 54(3): 357–358.

Crowley, Sharon. 1998. *Composition in the University: Historical and Polemical Essays.* Pittsburgh, PA: University of Pittsburgh Press.

Crowley, Sharon, and Deborah Hawhee. 2003. *Ancient Rhetorics for Contemporary Students.* Boston, MA: Pearson.

Cullum, Linda. 2000. "Surprised by Service: Creating Connections Through Community-Based Writing." *Reflections* 1(2): 5–11.

Cushman, Ellen. 2002b. "Sustainable Service Learning Programs." *College Composition and Communication* 54(1): 40–65.

———. 1998. *The Struggle and the Tools: Oral and Literate Strategies in an Inner City Community.* Albany, NY: SUNY Press.

———. 1999. "The Public Intellectual, Service Learning and Activist Research." *College English* 61(3): 328–336.

———. 2002a. "Service Learning as the New English Studies." In *Beyond English, Inc: Curricular Reform in a Global Economy.* David Downing, Claude Mark Hurlbert, and Paula Mathieu, eds. Portsmouth, NH: Boynton/Cook Heinemann.

Cushman, Ellen, and Chalon Emmons. "Contact Zones Made Real." In *School's Out: Bridging Out-of-School Literacies with Classroom Practice.* Glynda Hull and Katherine Schultz, eds. New York: Teachers College Press, 2002. 203–232.

Cvetovich, Ann, and Douglas Kellner, eds. 1997. *Articulating the Global and the Local: Globalization and Cultural Studies.* Boulder, CO: Westview Press.

Czajkowski, Fran. 20 August 2003. Personal interview.

Daniel, Jamie Owen, and Tom Moylan, eds. 1997. *Not Yet: Reconsidering Ernst Bloch.* London: Verso.

Deans, Thomas. 2000a. "CCCC Institutionalizes Service-Learning (Interview)." *Reflections* 1(1): 3–4.

———. 2000b. *Writing Partnerships: Service-Learning in Composition.* Urbana, IL: National Council of Teachers of English.

———. "Community Service and Critical Teaching: A Retrospective Conversation with Bruce Herzberg." *Reflections* 3(1): 71–76.

Desjarlais, Robert. 1997. *Shelter Blues: Sanity and Selfhood Among the Homeless.* Philadelphia, PA: University of Pennsylvania Press.

Deutsche, Rosyln. 1996. *Evictions: Art and Spatial Politics.* Cambridge, MA: MIT Press.

Di Leo, Jeffrey R., Walter Jacobs, and Amy Lee. 2002. "The Sites of Pedagogy." *Symploke* 10(1–2): 7–12.

Dobrin, Sidney I., and Christian Weisser, eds. 2001. *Ecocomposition: Theoretical and Pedagogical Approaches.* Albany, NY: SUNY Press.

Dorman, Wade, and Susan Fox Dorman. 1997. "Service Learning: Bridging the Gap Between the Real World and the Composition Classroom." In *Writing the Community: Concepts and Models for Service-Learning in Composition.* Linda Adler-Kassner, Robert Crooks, and Ann Watters, eds. Washington, D.C.: American Association for Higher Education Press. 119–133.

Douglas, Mary. 1991. "Jokes." *Rethinking Popular Culture.* Edited by Chandra Mukerji and Michael Schudson. Los Angeles: University of California Press.

Downing, David. 2002. "Beyond Disciplinary English: Integrating Reading and Writing by Reforming Academic Labor." In *Beyond English, Inc: Curricular Reform in a Global Economy.* David Downing, Claude Mark Hurlbert, and Paula Mathieu, eds. Portsmouth, NH: Boynton/Cook Heinemann. 23–38.

Downing, David, Claude Mark Hurlbert, and Paula Mathieu, eds. 2002. *Beyond English, Inc: Curricular Reform in a Global Economy.* Portsmouth, NH: Boynton/Cook Heinemann.

Downing, David, and James Sosnoski, eds. 1997. *Conversations in Honor of James Berlin, Works and Days* 27/28.

Duffy, Cheryl Hofstetter. 2003. "Tapping the Potential of Service-Learning: Guiding Principles for Redesigning Our Composition Courses." *Reflections* 3(1):1–13.

Eberly, Rosa. 1999. "From *Writers, Audiences,* and *Communities* to *Publics:* Writing Classrooms as Protopublic Spaces." *Rhetoric Review* 18(1):165–178.

Eighner, Lars. 1994. *Travels with Lizbeth.* New York: Random House.

Elbow, Peter. 1991. "Reflections on Academic Discourse: How It Relates to Freshman and Colleagues." *College English* 53(2): 135–155.

Ellis, David. 1991. "Actors with Dirty Faces." *Time.* 137(3): 19.

Emig, Janet. 1971. *The Composing Processes of Twelfth Graders.* Urbana, IL: National Council of Teachers of English.

Emig, Janet with Louise Wetherbee Phelps. 1995. Introduction. *Feminine Principles and Women's Experience in American Composition and Rhetoric.* Ed. Louise Wetherbee Phelps and Janet Emig. Pittsburgh, PA: U of Pittsburgh Press. xi–xviii.

Epstein, Deborah, and Paula Mathieu, eds. 2000. *This is My Job: Writings by the StreetWise Writers Group.* Issue of the *Journal of Ordinary Thought* 10(2).

Ervin, Elizabeth. 1997. "Encouraging Civic Participation Among First Year Writing Students, or Why Composition Class Should be More Like a Bowling Team." *Rhetoric Review* 15: 382–399.

Farmer, Frank. 2002. "Community Intellectuals." *College English* 65(2): 202–210.

Feldman, Ann. 2002. "Teaching Writing in a Context of Partnership." In *City Comp: Identities, Spaces, Practices.* Bruce McComiskey and Cynthia Ryan, eds. Albany, NY: SUNY Press. 203–215.

Feldman, Ann, Nancy Downs, and Ellen McManus, eds. 2002. *In Context: Participating in Cultural Conversations.* New York: Pearson.

Ferguson, Charles. 28 May 2004. Personal interview.

Fish, Stanley. 21 May 2004. "Why We Built the Ivory Tower." *New York Times,* 23.

The Fisher King. 1991. Directed by Terry Gilliam. Columbia Pictures.

Fitzpatrick, Stella. 1995. "Sailing Out from Safe Harbours: Writing for Publishing in Adult Basic Education." In *Literacy, Language and Community Publishing: Essays in Adult Education.* Jane Mace, ed. Clevedon, UK; Philadelphia, PA: Multilingual Matters, 1995. 1–22.

Flower, Linda. 1997. "Partners in Inquiry: A Logic for Community Outreach." In *Writing the Community: Concepts and Models for Service-Learning in Composition.* Linda Adler-Kassner, Robert Crooks, and Ann Watters, eds. Washington, D.C.: American Association for Higher Education Press. 95–119.

———. 2003. "Talking Across Difference: Intercultural Rhetoric and the Search for Situated Knowledge." *College Composition and Communication.* 55(1): 38–68.

Flower, Linda, Elenore Long, and Lorraine Higgins. 2000. *Learning to Rival: A Literate Practice for Intercultural Inquiry.* Mayhew, NJ: Lawrence Erlbaum.

Ford, Marjorie, and Elizabeth Schave. 2002. *Community Matters.* New York: Pearson.

Freire, Paulo. 1997. *Pedagogy of the Oppressed.* Translated by Myra Bergman Ramos. New York: Continuum.

Furco, Andrew. 2003. "Self-Assessment Rubric for the Institutionalization of Service Learning in Higher Education (Revised 2003)." Campus Compact at Brown University. http://www.tulane.edu/~ServLrng/Rubric_Background_rev2003.doc.

Gallagher, Chris. 2002. *Radical Departures: Composition and Progressive Pedagogy.* Urbana, IL: National Council of Teachers of English.

Gayfer, Margaret. 1995. "Introduction," Mace 2–15.

George, Diana. 2002. "The Word on the Street: Public Discourse in a Culture of Disconnect." *Reflections* 2(2): 5–18.

———. 2003. "A Matter of Life and Death: Public Debate in a Culture of Consent." *College Composition and Communication* 52(2): 345–348.

———. 2004. "The People's Power in the Small Press." *Hospitality* 23(6):1.

———. 5 June 2004. Personal interview.

George, Diana, and John Trimbur. 1995. *Reading Culture.* New York: Harper Collins.

Gere, Anne Ruggles. 1994. "Kitchen Tables and Rented Rooms: The Extracurriculum of Composition." *College Composition and Communication* 45(1): 75–92.

Gilyard, Keith, ed. 1999. *Race, Rhetoric and Composition.* Portsmouth, NH: Boynton/Cook Heinemann.

Goldblatt, Eli, and Stephen Parks. 2000. "Writing Beyond the Curriculum: Fostering New Collaborations in Literacy." *College English* 62(5): 584–606.

Goldfinger, Marc. D. 2003. *Relationships.* Cambridge, MA: Ibbetson Street Press.

———. 26 January 2004. Personal interview.

Goodburn, Amy. 2001. "Writing the Public Sphere through Family/Community History." *Readerly/Writerly Texts* 9(1–2): 9–24.

Goodman, Lorie J. 1998. "Just Serving/Just Writing." *Composition Studies* 26(1): 59–71.

Green, Ann. 2003. "Difficult Stories: Service-Learning, Race, Class and Whiteness." *College Composition and Communication.* 55(2): 276–301.

Grisham, John. 1998. *The Street Lawyer.* New York: Random House.

Gugerty, Catherine R., and Erin D. Swezey. 1996. "Developing Campus-Community Relationships." In *Service Learning in Higher Education: Concepts and Practices.* Hoboken, NJ: Wiley.

Hairston, Maxine. 1992. "Diversity, Ideology and Teaching Writing." *College Composition and Communication* 43(2): 179–193.

Harkin, Patricia. 2002. "Game and Earnest in Curricular Reform." Conference on College Composition and Communication.

Harper, Todd M., Emily Donnelli, and Frank Farmer. 2003. "Wayward Inventions: He(u)retical Experiments in Theorizing Service Learning." *Journal of Advanced Composition* 23(3): 615–640.

Harris, Joseph. 1996. *A Teaching Subject: Composition Since 1966.* Boston, MA: Pearson.

Harris, Tim. 24 July 2003. Personal interview.

Harvey, David. 1989. *The Condition of Postmodernity.* Oxford, UK: Blackwell.

————. 2000. *Spaces of Hope*. Berkeley, CA: University of California Press.

Hawisher, Gail, and Cynthia Selfe, eds. 1999. *Passions, Pedagogies, Technologies*. Urbana, IL: National Council of Teachers of English.

Hayler, Michael, and Alistair Thomson. 1995. "Working with Words: Active Learning in a Community Writing and Publishing Group." In *Literacy, Language and Community Publishing: Essays in Adult Education*. Jane Mace, ed. Clevedon, UK; Philadelphia, PA: Multilingual Matters, 1995. 42–59.

Heath, Shirley Brice. 1983. *Ways with Words: Language, Life and Work in Communities and Classrooms*. New York: Cambridge University Press.

Heilker, Paul. 1997. "Rhetoric Made Real: Civic Discourse and Writing Beyond the Curriculum." In *Writing the Community: Concepts and Models for Service-Learning in Composition*. Linda Adler-Kassner, Robert Crooks, and Ann Watters, eds. Washington, D.C.: American Association for Higher Education Press. 71–78.

Heller, Carolyn. 1997. *Until We Are Strong Together: Women Writers in the Tenderloin*. New York: Teachers College Press.

Hessler, H. Brooke. 2000. "Composing an Institutional Identity: The Terms of Community Service in Higher Education." *Language and Learning Across the Disciplines* 4(3): 27–42.

Herzberg, Bruce. 1994. "Community Service and Critical Teaching." *College Composition and Communication* 45(3): 307–319.

————. 2000. "Service Learning and Public Discourse." *Journal of Advanced Composition* 20(2): 393–404.

Himley, Margaret. 2004. "Facing (Up To) 'The Stranger' in Community Service Learning." *College Composition and Communication* 55(3): 416–438.

hooks, bell. 2000. *All about Love*. New York: William Morrow.

Howard Zinn: You Can't Be Neutral on a Moving Train. 2004. Directed by Deb Ellis and Denis Mueller. First Run Features.

Hull, Glynda, and Katherine Schultz, eds. 2002. *School's Out: Bridging Out-of-School Literacies with Classroom Practice*. New York: Teachers College Press.

Hurlbert, C. Mark, and Michael Blitz, eds. 1991. *Composition and Resistance*. Portsmouth, NH: Boynton/Cook.

Hurlbert, C. Mark, and Samuel Totten. 1992. *Social Issues in the English Classroom*. Urbana, IL: National Council of Teachers of English.

Hutchinson, Patricia. 2002. "Service Learning: Challenges and Opportunities." New Foundations: Organizational Issues and Insights. http://www.newfoundations.com/OrgTheory/Hutchinson721.html.

Isaacs, Emily J., and Phoebe Jackson. 2001. *Public Works: Student Writing as Public Text*. Portsmouth, NH: Boynton/Cook Heinemann.

It Was a Wonderful Life. 1993. Directed by Michèle Ohayon. Ridgbury Films.

Jahiel, René, ed. 1992. *Homelessness: A Prevention-Oriented Approach*. Baltimore, MD: Johns Hopkins Press.

Jameson, Fredric. 1998. "Cognitive Mapping." In *Marxism and the Interpretation of Culture*. Edited by Cary Nelson and Lawrence Grossberg. Chicago, IL: University of Illinois Press.

"Jane." 17 June 2004. Personal interview.

Jencks, Christopher. 1994. *The Homeless*. Cambridge, MA: Harvard University Press.

Julier, Laura. 2001. "Community Service Pedagogy." In *Guide to Composition Pedagogies*. Edited by Gary Tate, Amy Rupiper, and Kurt Schick. New York: Oxford University Press.

Kendrick, J. Richard, and John Suarez. 2003. "Service-Learning Outcomes in English Composition Courses: An Application of the Campus Compact Assessment Protocol." *Reflections* 3(1): 36–54.

Kress, Gunther. 1999. "English at the Crossroads." In *Passions, Pedagogies, Technologies*. Gail Hawisher, and Cynthia Selfe, eds. Urbana, IL: National Council for Teachers of English, 1999. 66–88.

Julier, Laura. 2001. "Community-Service Pedagogy." *A Guide to Composition Pedagogy*. eds. Gary Tate, Amy Rupiper, and Kurt Schick. New York: Oxford University Press.

Lawson, Linda. (2001) "Following Nancy Home." *Fourth Genre* 3:2. 162–174.

Levitas, Ruth. 1997. "Educated Hope: Ernst Bloch on Abstract and Concrete Utopia." In *Not Yet: Reconsidering Ernst Bloch*. Jamie Owen Daniel and Tom Moylan, eds. London: Verso. 65–79.

Levy, Ze'ev. 1997. "Utopia and Reality in the Philosophy of Ernst Bloch." In *Not Yet: Reconsidering Ernst Bloch*. Jamie Owen Daniel and Tom Moylan, eds. London: Verso. 175–185.

Loeb, Paul Rogat. 1999. *Soul of a Citizen: Living with Conviction in a Cynical Time*. New York: St. Martin's Press.

Mace, Jane, ed. 1995. *Literacy, Language and Community Publishing: Essays in Adult Education*. Clevedon, UK; Philadelphia, PA: Multilingual Matters.

Mack, Nancy. 2002."The Ins, Outs and In-Betweens of Multigenre Writing." *English Journal* 92(2): 91–98.

Maclean, Lisa. 4 April 2003. Personal interview.

Mahoney, Megan. 10 May 2004. Personal interview.

Malinowitz, Harriet. 1995. *Textual Orientations: Lesbian and Gay Students and the Making of Discourse Communities*. Portsmouth, NH: Boynton/Cook Heinemann.

Martin, Michael John. 2000. "Merging Voices: University Students Writing with Children in a Public Housing Project." *Reflections* 1(1): 14–17.

Mathieu, Paula. 1999. "Economic Citizenship and the Rhetoric of Gourmet Coffee." *Rhetoric Review* 18(1):112–127.

———. 2003. "Not Your Mama's Bus Tour: A Case for 'Radically Insufficient' Writing." In *City Comp: Identities, Spaces, Practices*. Bruce McComiskey and Cynthia Ryan, eds. Albany, NY: SUNY Press. 71–84.

————. 2001. *Questions of Empowerment: Teaching Writing at a 'Homeless' Community Newspaper.* Ph.D. Dissertation. University of Illinois at Chicago. UMI Dissertation Services, Ann Arbor, MI.

Mathieu, Paula, George Grattan, Tim Lindgren, and Staci Shultz, eds. (forthcoming) *Writing Places.* Boston, MA: Pearson.

Mathieu, Paula, and James J. Sosnoski. 2002. "Enacting Cultures: The Practice of Comparative Cultural Study." In *The Relevance of English: Teaching that Matters in Students' Lives.* Robert P. Yagelski and Scott A. Leonard, eds. Urbana, IL: NCTE. 324–343.

Mathieu, Paula, James J. Sosnoski, and David Zauhar. 1998. "Cultural Studies." In *Theorizing Composition.* Edited by Mary Lynch Kennedy. Westport, CT: Greenwood Press.

Mathieu, Paula, Karen Westmoreland, Michael Ibrahem, William Plowman, and Curly Cohen. 2004. "Questions of Time: Publishing and Group Identity in the *StreetWise* Writers Group." In *Writing Groups Inside and Outside the Classroom.* Edited by Beverly J. Moss, Nels P. Highberg, and Melissa Nicolas. Mahwan, NJ: Lawrence Erlbaum Press. 151–168.

Mauriello, Nicholas, and Gian Pagnucci. 2001. "Can't We Just Xerox This? The Ethical Dilemma of Writing for the World Wide Web." In *Public Works: Student Writing as Public Text.* Emily J. Isaacs and Phoebe Jackson. Portsmouth, NH: Boynton/Cook Heinemann. 44–52.

McComiskey, Bruce. 2000. *Teaching Composition as a Social Process.* Logan, UT: Utah State University Press.

McComiskey, Bruce, and Cynthia Ryan, eds. 2003. *City Comp: Identities, Spaces, Practices.* Albany, NY: SUNY Press.

Min, Eungjin, ed. 1999. *Reading the Homeless: The Media's Image of Homeless Culture.* Westport, CT: Praeger.

Mintz, Suzanné D., and Garry W. Heisser. 1996. "Principles of Good Practice in Service-Learning." In *Service Learning in Higher Education: Concepts and Practices.* Hoboken, NJ: Wiley.

Moneyhun, Clyde. 2000. "God and Mammon in Community Literacy: The Dialectic of Service, Activism and Inquiry." Conference of College Composition and Communication.

Moran, Charles. 2001. "Public and Private Writing in the Information Age." In *Public Works: Student Writing as Public Text.* Emily J. Isaacs and Phoebe Jackson. Portsmouth, NH: Boynton/Cook Heinemann. 35–43.

Mortenson, Peter. 1998. "Going Public." *College Composition and Communication* 50(2): 182–205.

Moylan, Tom. 1986. *Demand the Impossible: Science Fiction and the Utopian Imagination.* New York: Methuen.

Murray, Donald. 1968. *A Writer Teaches Writing.* Boston, MA: Houghton Mifflin.

Muth, Marcia. 2004. *Community Voices: Academic, Work and Public Readings.* New York: Pearson.

Nardini, Gloria. 1999. *Che bella figura! The Power of Performance in an Italian Ladies' Club in Chicago*. Albany, NY: SUNY Press.

National Coalition for the Homeless. 2001. "How Many People Are Homeless?" http://www.nationalhomeless.org/numbers.htm.

Negt, Oskar, and Alexander Kluge. 1993. *The Public Sphere and Experience*. Minneapolis, MN: University of Minnesota Press, 1993.

Nelson, Cary. 2001. "What Hath English Wrought: The Corporate University's Fast-Food Discipline." http://www.workplace-gsc.com/features1/nelson.html.

———. 2002. "Between Anonymity and Celebrity: The Zero Degrees of Professional Identity." *College English* 64(6): 710–719.

Newkirk, Thomas. 1997. *The Performance of Self in Student Writing*. Portsmouth, NH: Heinemann.

O'Dair, Sharon. 2004. "Comment and Response: Sharon O'Dair Responds." *College English* 66(5): 563–565.

O'Flaherty, Brendan. 1996. *Making Room: The Economics of Homelessness*. Cambridge, MA: Harvard University Press.

O'Reilly, Mary Rose. 1993. *The Peaceable Classroom*. Portsmouth, NH: Boynton/Cook.

Owens, Derek. 2001. *Composition and Sustainability: Teaching for a Threatened Generation*. Urbana, IL: National Council of Teachers of English.

Pagnucci, Gian, and Nicholas Mauriello, eds. 2000. "The Future of Narrative Discourse: Internet Constructs of Literacy and Identity." *Works and Days*. Vols. 33–36.

Paretsky, Sara. 1998. *Ghost Country*. New York: Random House.

Peck, Wayne Campbell, Linda Flower, and Lorraine Higgins. 1995. "Community Literacy." *College Composition and Communication* 46(2): 199–222.

Penticoff, Richard, and Linda Brodkey. 1992. "Writing About Difference: Hard Cases for Cultural Studies." In *Cultural Studies in the English Classroom*. James Berlin and Michael Vivion, eds. Portsmouth, NH: Boynton, Cook/Heinneman. 123–144.

Petley, Julian, and Sheila McKechnie. 1993. "Why Cathy Will Never Come Home Again." *New Statesman & Society* 6(246):S23+.

Porter, James, Patricia Sullivan, Stuart Blythe, Jeffrey Grabill, and Libby Miles. 2000. "Institutional Critique: A Rhetorical Methodology for Change." *CCC* 51(4): 610–642.

Powell, Katrina M., and Pamela Takayoshi. 2003. "Accepting the Roles Created for Us: The Ethics of Reciprocity." *CCC* 54(3): 394–422.

Pratt, Mary Louise. 1991. "Arts of the Contact Zone." *Profession* MLA: 33–40.

Readings, Bill. 1996. *The University in Ruins*. Cambridge, MA: Harvard University Press.

Redd, Theresa. 2003. "In the Eye of the Beholder: Contrasting Views of Community Service Writing." *Reflections* 3(1): 14–31.

Reynolds, Nedra. 1998. "Composition's Imagined Geographies: The Politics of Space in the Frontier, City and Cyberspace." *CCC* 50(1): 12–35.

———. 2004. *Geographies of Writing: Inhabiting Places and Encountering Difference*. Carbondale, IL: Southern Illinois University Press.

Rumpf, Caesréa. 21 August 2000. "Vendors Take their Show on the Road." *StreetWise*, 14.

Sassen, Saskia. 2002. *The Global City: New York, London, Tokyo*. 2d ed. Princeton, NJ: Princeton University Press.

Sayer, Cathy. 2000. "Juggling Teacher Responsibilities in Service-Learning Courses." *Reflections* 1(1): 20–23.

Scapansky, Tim. 2004. "Service Learning and Faculty in the Higher Education Institution." New Foundations. Organizational Issues and Insights. http://www.newfoundations.com/OrgTheory/Scepansky721.htm.

Schiappa, Edward. 1995. "Intellectuals and the Place of Cultural Critique." In *Rhetoric, Cultural Studies and Literacy*. Edited by John Frederick Reynolds. Hillsdale, NJ: Lawrence Erlbaum.

Schmied, Harald. (2001). Personal email.

Schutz, Aaron, and Anne Ruggles Gere. 1998. "Service Learning and English Studies: Rethinking 'Public' Service." *College English* 60(2): 126–149.

Shareef, Reginald. 2000. "Roanoke's Blacks Deserve an Official Apology for Past." http://www.roanoke.com/magazine/shareef/092500.html.

Shor, Ira. 1996. *When Students Have Power: Negotiating Authority in a Critical Pedagogy*. Chicago, IL: University of Chicago Press.

Sirc, Geoffrey. 2002. *English Composition as a Happening*. Logan, UT: Utah State Press.

Smith, Paul. 1997. *Millennial Dreams: Contemporary Culture and Capital in the North*. London: Verso.

Sosnoski, James, Patricia Harkin, and Ann Feldman. 2002. "Collaborative Learning Networks: A Curriculum for the 21st Century." In *Beyond English, Inc: Curricular Reform in a Global Economy*. David Downing, Claude Mark Hurlbert, and Paula Mathieu, eds. Portsmouth, NH: Boynton/Cook Heinemann. 219–230.

Stark, Louisa. 1992. "Demographics and Stereotypes of Homeless People." In *Homelessness: A Prevention-Oriented Approach*. René Jahiel, ed. Baltimore, MD: Johns Hopkins Press. 27–39.

Street, Brian V. 1995. *Social Literacies: Critical Approaches to Literacy in Development Ethnography, and Education*. London; New York: Pearson.

Stringer, Lee. 1999. *Grand Central Winter: Stories from the Street*. New York: Washington Square Press.

Terkel, Studs. 2003. *Hope Dies Last: Keeping Faith in Difficult Times*. New York: New Press.

Tobin, Lad. 1994. "Introduction: How the Writing Process Was Born—and Other Conversion Narratives." In *Taking Stock: The Writing Process Movement in the '90s.* Edited by Lad Tobin and Thomas Newkirk. Portsmouth, NH: Boynton/Cook.

Trimbur, John. 2000. "Composition and the Circulation of Writing." *College Composition and Communication* 52(2): 188–219.

Trimbur, John, Robert G. Wood, Ron Strickland, William H. Thelin, William J. Rouster, Toni Mester, and Maxine Hairston. 1993. "Responses to Maxine Hairston, 'Diversity, Ideology and Teaching Writing' and Reply." *CCC* 44(2): 248–256.

Verburg, Carol J. 1997. *Making Contact: Readings from Home and Abroad.* Boston, MA: Bedford/St. Martin's.

Villanueva, Victor. 1993. *Bootstraps: From an American Academic of Color.* Urbana, IL: National Council of Teachers of English.

Vogell, Heather. 27 August 2000. "Bus Tour Takes a Ride on the Gritty Side: Program Explores Life via Street Theater." *Chicago Tribune*, 4:1+.

Weisser, Christian R. 2002. *Moving Beyond Academic Discourse: Composition Studies and the Public Sphere.* Carbondale, IL: Southern Illinois University Press.

Welch, Nancy. December 2002. "'And Now That I Know Them': Composing Mutuality in a Service Learning Course." *CCC* 52(2): 243–263.

Wells, Susan. 1996. "Rogue Cops and Health Care: What Do We Want from Public Writing?" *College Composition and Communication* 47(3): 325–341.

Williams, Raymond. 1976. *Keywords: A Vocabulary of Culture and Society.* London: Croon Helm.

With Honors. 1994. Directed by Alek Keshishian. Warner Brothers.

Yagelski, Robert P., and Scott A. Leonard, eds. 2002. *The Relevance of English: Teaching that Matters in Students' Lives.* Urbana, IL: National Council of Teachers of English.

Zebroski, James Thomas. 2002. "Composition and Rhetoric, Inc.: Life after the English Department at Syracuse University." In *Beyond English, Inc: Curricular Reform in a Global Economy.* David Downing, Claude Mark Hurlbert, and Paula Mathieu, eds. Portsmouth, NH: Boynton/Cook Heinemann. 164–180.

Zencey, Eric. 2001. "The Rootless Professors." Qtd. Owens, 72–73.

Zinn, Howard. 1994. *You Can Be Neutral on a Moving Train.* Boston, MA: Beacon Press.

———. 19 June 2004. Personal interview.

Zipes, Jack. 1997. "Traces of Hope: The Non-Synchronicity of Ernst Bloch." In *Not Yet: Reconsidering Ernst Bloch.* Jamie Owen Daniel and Tom Moylan, eds. London: Verso. 1–12.

Zlotkowski, Edward. 2000. "Service-Learning and Composition: As Good as It Gets (Interview)." *Reflections* 3(1): 1–3.

Index